La Civiltà Cattolica

The Jewish Question in Europe

LA CIVILTÀ CATTOLICA

THE JEWISH QUESTION IN EUROPE

Introduction by

E. Michael Jones

FIDELITY PRESS

South Bend, Indiana

2020

Published by FIDELITY PRESS in South Bend, Indiana
www.fidelitypress.org
574-289-9786
First Edition

All rights reserved. No part of this book may be reproduced, stored in a retrieval system, or transmitted in any form or by any means, electronic, mechanical, photocopying, recording or otherwise, without the prior permission of Fidelity Press.

Printed and bound in the United States of America
by St. Martin de Porres Dominican Community

E. Michael Jones, Ph.D.
    La Civiltà Cattolica: The Jewish Question in Europe
    ISBN: 978-0-929891-27-9

Part I: *La Civiltà Cattolica*, Series XIV, Vol. VII, *Fascicule* 961, 23 October 1890.
Part II: *La Civiltà Cattolica*, Series XIV, Vol. VIII, *Fascicule* 970, 4 November 1890.
Part III: *La Civiltà Cattolica*, Series XIV, Vol. VIII, *Fascicule* 972, 9 December 1890.

The Translator prefers to remain anonymous.

TABLE OF CONTENTS

Preface — ix

Introduction — 1

Part I: The Causes — 13

Part II: The Effects — 27

Part III: The Remedies — 45

From The Translator:

    Roman Numeral Notes — 57

    Translator's Note — 63

PREFACE

One hundred years after the French Revolution, the editors of *Civiltà Cattolica*, the official voice of the Vatican on political affairs, came to a startling conclusion: any country which turns away from laws based on the teaching of the Catholic Church and God's eternal law will end up being ruled by Jews. These three articles, originally published over the fall of 1890, explain in detail why this is so, for both France in 1890 and America today.

E. Michael Jones
South Bend, Indiana
February 2012

BY E. MICHAEL JONES

INTRODUCTION

At the end of Euripedes play The Bacchae[1], Cadmus asks his daughter Agave, "What do you see?" Agave is sitting center stage with the severed human head of her son Pentheus in her lap. Pentheus, King of Thebes, was torn limb from limb by the women of Thebes as they danced naked on the mountainside worshipping the Asiatic god Dionysos. Still intoxicated by the revelry that led to her son's death, Agave says, "it's a lion's head, a trophy for the palace." At this point, Cadmus says, "Look carefully. Study it more closely." As the intoxication wears off, Agave recognizes what she has done and answers, "I see horror. I see suffering. I see grief."

"Does it still look like a lion?" Cadmus asks

"No, Pentheus. I am holding his head."

"You were mad," Cadmus tells his daughter. "The city was possessed by Dionysos."

At this point, Agave awakes to the full consequence of her actions.

"I see now," she says, "Dionysos has destroyed us."

America went through its own bout of Dionysian intoxication in the days following May 25, 2020 when a Minneapolis cop by the name of Derek Chauvin knelt on the neck of a 46-year-old Black man by the name of George Floyd[2], causing his death. Corrupted by 66 years of bad education, America's Black Lumpenproletariat erupted in an orgy of rioting[3] that brought the rule of law to an end in many of America's large cities. The rioting was based on an incident, and the incident was captured in an image. What did Americans see

---

[1]. https://www.gutenberg.org/files/35173/35173-h/35173-h.htm
[2]. https://archive.is/wip/0vQMP
[3]. https://archive.is/Ls0qA

when they saw Officer Chauvin kneeling on George Floyd's neck? They saw racism.[4]

The Palestinians who watched the same video, however, saw something else. They recognized the knee hold that Officer Chauvin inflicted on Floyd as the same technique which Israeli police routinely used on Palestinians. Missing from the mainstream account of Floyd's death was any mention of the role which the Anti-Defamation League[5] played in weaponizing the Minneapolis police department. The ADL has been pressuring police departments across the country for years[6] to train with Israeli instructors to learn submission techniques like the knee on the throat hold[7]. But more importantly, the policemen who are subjected to the Israelification of local police forces learn more than techniques. They learn attitudes, and the main attitude they learn is that they should treat their fellow citizens, the people who fund their local police departments with their tax money, in the same way that Israelis treat Palestinians.

If the image of Officer Chauvin kneeling on the neck of a black man symbolized white racism, then the image of George Floyd symbolized the black man as victim of that racism, and Black Lives Matter as his champion. But here appearances are deceiving because Jews are behind this side of the equation. During the time leading up to the riots in Ferguson, Missouri George Soros gave Black Lives Matter $33 million dollars.[8]

The ADL is involved on this side of the conflict as well. With Israel's annexation of the West Bank looming, the ADL is concerned that the backlash that the annexation is sure to cause, might spread to its proxy warriors in Black Lives Matter, as in fact did happen in England:[9]

> The "stakeholders analysis memo," which was issued by the ADL's Government Relations, Advocacy, and Community Engagement department and marked as a draft, warns that the group will need to find a way to defend Israel from criticism without alienating other civil rights organizations, elected officials of color, and Black Lives Matter activists and supporters. The memo suggests that the group hopes to avoid appearing openly hostile to public criticism of annexation while it works to block legislation that harshly censures

---

[4]. https://archive.is/wip/D0vpy
[5]. https://archive.is/nLGxT
[6]. https://archive.is/k14rA
[7]. https://archive.is/rtFhU
[8]. https://archive.is/ZnIYJ
[9]. https://archive.is/qrUuQ

Introduction

Israel or leads to material consequences, such as conditioning United States military support.[10]

The ADL was not the only Jewish organization supporting Black Lives Matter. According to a report in the Jewish Telegraph Agency, "More than 400 Jewish organizations and synagogues in the United States have signed on to a letter that asserts 'unequivocally: Black Lives Matter.'"[11] Those groups represented a broad spectrum "of religious, political, gender, and racial identities. The list of signatories — from small congregations to major Jewish organizations — represents millions of Jewish people in the United States, the organizers," according to the statement. What name do we give to this involvement? In America it was called the Black-Jewish alliance.

For the 70 years following the lynching of Leo Frank[12], Jewish organizations like the Anti-Defamantion League (ADL) and the National Association for the Advancement of Colored People, (NAACP), tried to foment race war in the United States. The culmination of this campaign came in the 1960s with the creation of the Civil Rights Movement. But the Jewish Revolutionary Spirit goes back farther than that. It goes back to the foot of the cross, when the Jewish High Priests Annas and Caiphas told Jesus that they would accept him as their Messiah if he came down from the cross and created the earthly kingdom they wanted. He didn't do that, and the Jews chose Barabbas instead. By rejecting Christ as their Messiah, the Jews rejected the Logos incarnate, and when they rejected the Logos they rejected the order God created for this universe, and when they rejected that, they became revolutionaries, which is what they are today in places like St. Louis.

St. Louis, Missouri was founded in 1764 by two French fur traders, Pierre Laclede and Auguste Chouteau and named after King Louis IX of France. Over the course of the 19th century it became the home to many Catholic immigrants from Ireland and Germany.[13] Many Frenchmen fought against the revolution. They were known as les Chouans and their uprising was known as the Vendeé. Some Frenchmen left France to escape the revolution. Many of them came to America, to cities like Quebec and Montreal in Canada, but also to cities like New Orleans and St. Louis in America. They did this to escape the revolution, but now the revolution has followed their descendants to places like St. Louis.

---

[10]. https://archive.is/7FtVI
[11]. https://archive.is/c36la
[12]. Cf. Jones, *The Jewish Revolutionary Spirit*, p. 693 ff.
[13]. https://en.wikipedia.org/wiki/St._Louis

The Jewish Question in Europe

A man by the name of Umar Lee wants to tear down the statue of St. Louis IX and rename the city, Confluence.[14] As in Minneapolis, appearances are deceptive. Lee claims to be a Muslim.[15] He also claims to have the support of Black Lives Matter, but why should they hold a grudge against a French king from the 13th century? Did Louis IX own black slaves? Did he have secret cotton plantations in Paris? No, Louis IX's crime was that he burned the Talmud.

Do the Blacks care about the Talmud? Do they know what it is? Do they know about the blasphemies it contains, which was the real reason it was burned? Probably not. As in Minneapolis, the group behind the protest is invisible. The Jewish revolutionary spirit is behind the protests in both cities. The battle in St. Louis is between Catholics and Jews, but Umar Lee, as front man for the Jews[16], must disguise this fact, and turn the conflict into a battle between blacks and whites.[17] This is a form of identity theft. It also leads to violence because once a group has white identity imposed upon it, the people in that group no longer have the right to free speech or assembly. This is precisely what happened in St. Louis.

After Umar Lee turned a group of Catholics who had assembled to pray the Rosary in defense of the statue into white people, Black Lives Matter showed up and felt entitled to beat up a 60 year old Catholic who was trying to pray the Rosary, because white people have no rights. The Revolution of 2020 in America is similar to the French Revolution because when the revolution came to France in 1789, Jewish involvement was not apparent.

Abbe Agustin Barruel suppressed the Simonini letter[18], which proved Jewish involvement, when he wrote his *Memoirs Illustrating the History of Jacobinism* and he exonerated the Whigs who used their weaponized Masonic lodges to bring down the Bourbon monarchy and unleash first anarchy and then tyranny in France. Jewish involvement in the French Revolution didn't become apparent until Napoleon emancipated the Jews in 1806.

In 1890, *Civiltà* Cattolica, the official magazine of the Vatican, did a three-part series on the Jewish Question in France one century after the French Revolution. Their conclusion was simple but stunning. Any country which turned away from laws created by Christian kings, as the French had done in 1789, would end up being ruled by Jews.

Civiltà Cattolica published its first issue on April 6, 1850. The founder of the review was a young Jesuit by the name of Carlo Maria Curci, who

---

[14]. https://archive.is/wip/mhgdL
[15]. https://archive.is/wip/mhgdL
[16]. https://archive.is/wip/mhgdL
[17]. https://archive.is/ufrt0
[18]. Cf. Jones, *Barren Metal* pp 1171

Introduction

justified the creation of a new journal by claiming that European journalism was "the child of the French revolution, intent on propagating blasphemous and anti-Christian ideas soaked in a rationalism which was both agnostic and atheistic."[19]

The Jesuits who founded *Civiltà Cattolica* were not acting on their own. The new magazine was created under the auspices of Pope Pius IX and viewed by him as the application of his anti-modernist theories, as expressed in the Syllabus of Errors, to the political situation of his day. *Civiltà* was to be a bulwark against modernist thought. It would allow the Church to combat the enemies of the Church with their own weapons. *Civiltà* took on "the avarice and pride of an ugly monk in Germany, the insatiable libido of a tyrant king in England, and the cult of national unity and independence which was promoted by all sorts of demagogues in Italy,"[20] and it did so with the approval of the pope. *Civiltà Cattolica* was conceived as an instrument in the Church's intellectual apostolate, and its scope was essentially apologetic and polemical. *Civiltà* distinguished itself from the moment of its inception in a series of battles against revolutionary thought, above all against liberalism, laicism and against the principles which were the inspiration for the French Revolution.[21]

The pope's support was both spiritual and financial. In February 1850, Pius IX, while still residing Naples, ordered Cardinal Antonelli to transfer 1,250 ducats from the pope's account at the Rothschild bank in Naples to the Jesuits and declared his willingness to take on whatever financial burdens necessary to ensure the successful launching of the review.[22] The great care the pope took in the launching of the magazine paid off when on March 20, subscriptions had reached 3,000. During the first three months of publication that number would jump to 6,307.[23]

The ties between *Civiltà* and the pope only became closer when Pius IX returned to Rome. From that point onward, "*Civiltà Cattolica* was considered as an expression of the voice of the Vatican, as well as a faithful interpreter

---

[19]. *Segregazione*, p. 3 "Curci descriveva il giornalismo europeo come figlio della rivoluzione francese, intento a difondere idee blasfeme e anticristiane, imbevute di razionalismo agnostico e ateo."
[20]. *Segregazione*, p. 3. "In Alemagna, fu l'avarizia e l'orgogio di un frate laido; in Inghilterra fu la insaziabile libidine di un re tiranno; in Italia dovrebb' essere l'unita e l'independenz nazionale intese alla maniera dei demogoghi."
[21]. *Segregazione*, p. 3. "La revista fu concepita come uno strumento di apostolato intelletuale e i suoi scopi erano essenzialmente apologetici e polemici. Fin dai suoi esordi si distinse sopratutto in una serie di battaglie a tutto campo rivolte sopratutto contro il liberalismo, il laicismo e i principi inspiratori della rivoluzione francese."
[22]. *Segregazione*, p. 4.
[23]. *Segregazione*, p. 4.

of the thought of the pope, which was well-research and intellectually superior."[24] On February 12, 1866, the pope, pleased by the success of the magazine, granted canonical status to the editorial staff at *Civiltà* by establishing the "Collegium Societatis Iesu Scriptorum Ephemeridi vulgo *La Civiltà Cattolica*" and granting them the privileges of other colleges of the society. From this moment on, only the pope could intervene in their affairs. As a result of this approval, *Civiltà Cattolica* soon became the most authoritative offical organ of the papacy, a status which not even the founding of *L'Osservatore Romano* in 1861 could undermine.[25] Both Pius IX and Leo XIII placed a very special trust ("*una fiducia tutta particolare*") in the Jesuits responsible for the magazine, and they reciprocated by returning that trust with a loyalty that was both absolute and deferential ("*con una fedelta assolute e deferente*").[26]

The birth of *Civiltà* coincided with the restoration of the ghetto under Pius IX, but in its early years the magazine did not devote any particular attention to the "Jewish problem."[27] In 1869 Pius IX praised and blessed Gougenot des Mosseau's book *Le Juif, let Judaism des peuples chrétiens et le judaisation*, which described the Talmud as "a savage code in which the precepts of hate and rapaciousness are mixed up with the magic doctrines of the caballah, a book which professes the greatest idolatry imaginable."[28]

Pope Pius IX died on February 7, 1878, just as the wave of anti-Jewish sentiment was beginning to break over all of Europe, beginning in France. One of the causes of that wave of anti-Jewish sentiment (or one of the manifestations of it) was the blood libel trials which sprang up in places like Hungary and later in Russia. Taradel and Raggi hold *Civiltà* as somehow responsible for this phenomenon by the very fact that they reported on it. They make it clear that from their point of view anyone who took the blood libel accusations seriously was guilty of anti-Semitism.

A similar view was expressed by Cardinal Vaughn and Lord Russell when they wrote to the head of the Holy Office in 1900 asking him to prohibit Catholics from mentioning the blood libel. The biting response of the Holy Office makes it clear that this request was tantamount to forbidding Catholics from talking about the O.J. Simpson trial because the blood libel was part of the legal history of countries like Poland and Bohemia and the Holy Office had no power to expunge those cases from the legal record. "Given all of this, the Holy See cannot give the declaration which has been requested, for

---

[24]. *Segregazione*, p. 4.
[25]. *Segregazione*, p. 6.
[26]. *Segregazione*, p. 7.
[27]. *Segregazione*, p. 10.
[28]. *Segregazione*, p. 11.

Introduction

even if it satisfied a few deluded Englishmen, it would give rise to protests and scandals elsewhere."[29] Taradal and Raggi claim that "the triumph of the *Civiltà Cattolica* line could not have been more complete. . . . The resolution of the Holy Office, under this point of view should come as no surprise: it is inconceivable that it would condemn publicly all of the blood libel accusations which had been promoted by the secretary of state and Leo XIII himself."[30]

The authors' indignation rings hollow today. In the eleven years which have lapsed since the publication of *La Segregazione amichevole*, we have seen the publication of Peter Schaeffer's book on Jesus and the Talmud, as well as the publication (subsequently withdrawn under Jewish pressure) of *Pasqua di Sangue*, a book substantiating the authenticity of the blood libel accusations written by Elio Toaff, the son of the former chief rabbi in Rome. In light of publications like this, *Civiltà Cattolica* seems more relevant to our age than the indignation of the defenders of the Enlightenment, defenders who deny legal facts on a priori grounds.

Civiltà Cattolica posited a chain of premises linked in logical fashion. The principles of the French Revolution have had a number of negative effects, the most pernicious of which was the emancipation of the Jews, which permitted them to do harm to the people who so recklessly granted them equal rights. That is largely because the Judaism of the past and the Judaism of the present are two completely different things.[31] Judaism as it exists now is satanic in its hatred of Christ and the Church. Taradel and Raggi fault *Civiltà Cattolica* for representing Judaism as the "demonic antitype of Christianity. . . . If the foundation of Christianity is love of neighbor, the foundation of Judaism can only be hatred elevated to a supreme religious precept."[32] The indignation on the part of the authors is palpable but misplaced. Since the publication of *La Segregazione amichevole*, a rabbi published an article in the America neoconservative journal *First Things*, explaining how hatred was a Jewish virtue.

Civiltà Cattolica's concern with the Jewish question reached its culmination during the reign of Pope Leo XIII. In 1890, one year after the hundredth anniversary of the French Revolution, Father Raffaele Ballerini wrote

---

[29]. *Segregazione*, p. 40. Stanti tutto cio la Santa Sede non puo dare la chiesta dichiarazione, la quale se contenterebbe i pochi illusi d'Inghiterra, solleverebbe proteste e scandal per tutto altrove.'
[30]. *Segregazione*, p. 44. 44 La risoluzione de Santo Uffizio, sotto questo punto da vista, no puo certo stupire: e inimmaginablie che potesse condannare pubblicamente, assieme all'accusa del sangue, la campagna promossa dalla CC con il tacito, ma evidente appogio dell segretaria di State e dello stess Leone XIII.
[31]. *Segregazione*, p. 20.
[32]. *Segregazione*, p. 21. il fondamento dell'ebraismo non puo che essere l'odio elevato a supremo precetto religioso.

7

anonymously a three part series on the Jewish question. That situation had changed under the reign of Pope Leo XIII. Behind the French Revolution, Pius IX saw Freemasonry; now behind Freemasonry, Leo XIII saw the Jews. In a sense the situation had to change because by the 1880s all of Europe had become obsessed with the Jewish question. If *Civiltà* was created to deal with current political issues, it had no choice but to deal with the Jewish question. As we have already indicated, Leo XIII saw this series as an antidote to the anti-Semitic fanaticism which was appearing in the Catholic Observer in Milan. Oblivious to their own explanation of Leo XIII's anti-anti-Semitism, Taradel and Raggi go on to claim that the 1890 *Civiltà* articles on the Jewish Question, "do not constitute, as is commonly thought, the moment of initiation of the anti-Semitic campaign but rather the point of its arrival."[33] According to the Jewish view of history, the Church was infected with anti-Semitism from the moment of its inception. But after 1900 years of persecuting the Jews, God went up the chimney at Auschwitz, and the Holocaust has replaced the crucifixion as the center of human history. To say that large parts of the Catholic world have been infected by this hermeneutic would not be an exaggeration. In their critique of *Civiltà Cattolica*, Taradel and Raggi even go so far as to say that anyone who felt that Jews were practitioners of predatory finance or supporters of revolution suffers from mental illness: "The obsession with a Jewish bolshevik plot, which has been defined by Norman Cohn as a true collective psychopathology became [at *Civiltà Cattolica*] the key to understanding all of the political events in Europe. . . . The myth of a Jewish conspiracy is the motor as well as the ideological lens through which *Civiltà Cattolica* explained to its readers history as it was unfolding."[34]

Like *Civiltà*, Georg Ratzinger, the great uncle of Pope Benedict XVI, traced Jewish hegemony in finance to the French Revolution. Following Napoleon's emancipation of the Jews, Jews took over the economies of one nation after another in Europe because of their sharp business practices. What Ratzinger calls "*Jüdisches Erwerbsleben*" allowed them to cheat the Christian natives, who had been taught to work hard, be trusting, and love their neighbor. Jewish immorality in finance, in other words, gave the Jews an unfair economic advantage in Catholic countries:

> The emancipation of the Jews, whose views and concepts contradicted the laws and customs of the Christian nations, could not help but have a destructive and corrupting effect on the entire Christian society. . . . This fact alone explains why Jews are able to accumulate

[33]. *Segregazione*, p. 28.
[34]. Ruggero Taradeland Barbara Raggi, (La Segregazione amichevole: "*La Civiltà Cattolica*" e la questin ebraica 1850-1945). (Roma: Editori Riuniti, 2000), p. 21.

riches so quickly. . . . The example of moral corruption has a contagious effect, and that explains the corrupting effect of Jewish influence on commerce.[35]

Ratzinger claimed that it was an act of supreme foolishness when the necessary protections for the social order were lifted in the years following 1789. Once this happened, it was only a matter of time before the Jews would gain the upper hand because the business ethics they derived from their study of the Talmud taught them that cheating the goyim was a virtue. This was particularly the case among the benevolent peoples who made up the population of Catholic nations, who had been taught to work hard and trust civil authority as defending their interests. Once these people fell into the hands of the usurers, they found they could not extricate themselves from its tentacles, in spite of their frugality. Because of the widespread acceptance of usury in the period following the French Revolution, just about everyone was impoverished, and only the Jews got rich. [36]

Ratzinger's book appeared in 1892, shortly following the publication of *Rerum Novarum*, Pope Leo XIII's encyclical on the condition of the working classes, and the three-part series in *Civiltà Cattolica* which warned Catholics about "the voracious octopus of Judaism."[37] The anger at Jewish business practices had reached the boiling point because those involved in the "lucrative professions" could amass riches at the cost of others in a few short years.[38]

That is the situation we find ourselves in today. America is in the middle of a revolution. As in Russia in 1917, where the revolution succeeded, and Germany in 1919, where it was thwarted, and even as in China, where the Cultural Revolution of 1966 was led by Jews like Sidney Rittenberg[39], Jews play the major role in the American cultural revolution of 2020. George Soros is one of those Jews.

After helping to create color revolutions in virtually every country which separated from the Soviet Union, Soros is creating a "colored" revolution in the United States, with the help of groups like Antifa[40], which has Jewish roots[41] going all the way back to Germany in the 1930s, and Black Lives Matter.

---

[35]. Waldhausen, Robert (Georg Ratzinger) *Jüdisches Erwerbsleben*: Skizzen aus dem sozialen Leben der Gegenwart (Passau: Verlag von Rudolf Abt, 1892) p. 2.
[36]. Ratzinger, *Jüdisches Erwerbsleben, p. 2.*
[37]. "The Jewish Question In Europe Part III: The Remedies" *La Civiltà Cattolica*, (Fidelity Press 2020).
[38]. Ratzinger, *Jüdisches Erwerbsleben*, p. 3.
[39]. Martin, David, "Sidney Rittenberg: The Jew Behind Communist China" *Culture Wars* Nov. 2019 (Vol. 38 #11)
[40]. https://archive.is/1QyAJ
[41]. https://archive.is/wip/3cCWV

The Jewish Question in Europe

Soros has also taken over large segments of local government by backing candidates for office with money from the Open Society Foundation.[42] Circuit Attorney Kim Gardner is one of those candidates.

Gardner has crippled law enforcement in St. Louis by enforcing the law based on the color of the citizen. After one year in office, Gardner let it be known she would not prosecute marijuana crimes.[43] In fact, in 2019 Gardner prosecuted only 1,000 of the over 7,000 cases the St. Louis Police Department submitted to her for prosecution.[44] She then drove the governor from office and filed charges against the St. Louis Police Department under the Ku Klux Klan act of 1965 accusing them of being a racist conspiracy.[45]

The Gardner-Soros connection is one of the best examples of the revival of the Black-Jewish Alliance after its demise in 1967.

Gardner also threatened to press charges against a Mark and Patricia McClocksey, who defended their house with firearms[46] after the police refused to respond to their call, when a black mob broke into their gated community. The outcome of the current revolution is uncertain at this moment. One of the main reasons for pessimism is the attitude of the Catholic Church toward its own saints and its own people.

Outgoing bishop Robert Carlson has defended the statue[47], but his successor, Mitchell Rozansky, of Springfield, Massachusetts has yet to take a position on the issue.[48] Since Rozansky is known as a proponent of Catholic-Jewish dialogue[49] and a protégé of the notorious judophile Cardinal Keeler of Baltimore[50], prospects for confronting the group responsible for the revolutionary vandalism in St. Louis look dim at best. We are now in a situation similar to the one which prevailed in the mid-to-late 1970s, when one country after another fell to communism.

That situation changed in the *annus mirabilis* of 1979[51] when the Ayatollah Khomeini led the overthrow of American materialism in Iran in February, and Pope John Paul II led a similar uprising against Marxist materialism in Poland four months later. The same type of spiritual revolution can save the situation now, but only if the Church abandons the failed experiment known

---

[42]. https://www.foxnews.com/politics/da-soros-justice
[43]. https://bit.ly/2EKHIBp
[44]. https://archive.is/wip/gsFsw
[45]. https://archive.is/LhTj8
[46]. https://archive.is/wip/hu92h
[47]. https://archive.is/wip/uOJt4
[48]. https://archive.is/wip/eR5fj
[49]. https://archive.is/wip/BnqCA
[50]. https://archive.is/wip/WP6Za
[51]. Cf. Jones, *Logos Rising* (2020), pp. 657 ff.

Introduction

as Catholic-Jewish dialogue[52] and returns to her traditional teaching on the Jews.

The Jews need to be confronted with their sins, as St. Peter did in the Acts of the Apostles when he told them that they killed Christ. The contemporary version of that accusation would include Jewish participation in both political and sexual revolutions which have led to untold deaths under Marxism[53] and unprecedented moral corruption under Wilhelm Reich, the Jew who created the term sexual revolution.[54]

Success in the culture wars will involve working for the Jews' conversion, rather than begging in vain for their friendship and approval. It will involve asking the Jews of St. Louis if they agree with the revolutionary program[55] that Rabbi Susan Talve has endorsed.[56] The alternative is violence.

Like *Civiltà*'s series on the Jewish Question, Ratzinger ended his book with a warning of what would follow if his call for reform were not heeded. Like *Civiltà*'s warning, Ratzinger's found uncanny fulfillment less than 50 years in the future:

> A reaction against the jewification of our culture is now building momentum among the common man. That movement is hardly perceptible today, but it is going to grow like an avalanche. That movement would be irresistible at this very moment if it weren't lacking a leader.[57]

Just in case you didn't know, the German word for leader is *Füehrer*.

E. Michael Jones
South Bend, Indiana
September 2020

---

[52]. https://archive.is/z2mEE
[53]. Cf. Jones, *The Jewish Revolutionary Spirit.*
[54]. Cf. Jones, *Libido Dominandi.*
[55]. https://archive.is/wip/ZasHM
[56]. https://archive.is/wip/pQr7P
[57]. Ratzinger, *Jüdisches Erwerbsleben,* p. 84.

PART I

THE CAUSES

The nineteenth century will close upon Europe, leaving it in the grips of a very sad question, from which, in the twentieth century, there will possibly be such calamitous consequences that they will cause Europe to bring it to an end by a definitive resolution.[i] We mean the unhappy so-called *Semitic* question, which is better called the *Jewish question*, and intimately linked to the economic, moral, political, and religious conditions of Europe's Christianity.

How urgent it is at present and how much it is upsetting the major nations becomes evident from the collective outcry against the *invasion* of the Israelites into every sector of public and social life; from the associations having formed in France, Austria, Germany, England, Russia, Romania, and elsewhere in order to stop it; from the outcrys which are beginning to make themselves heard within the parliaments; finally, from the great number of newspapers, books, and pamphlets continuously appearing in order to point out the necessity of stopping and combating the spread of this plague, and stressing its most pernicious consequences.

For some time here in this review, we also have been dealing with the specific question, which is the social one, under more critical, historical, and scientific viewpoints, and have indicated the true causes of the lamentable effects that are now increasingly deplored. But the great number of publications which lately have come to our attention, among them some quite important ones, invites us to revert it by summarizing in a few pages the many aspects involved; and we think that it fully deserves to be considered in Italy where Judaism rules as lord but where, in spite of the rich material available, still no one has emerged to write a treatise that could compete with the respective one of Edouard Drumont and, as we believe, would be devoured with great profit.[1]

The Jewish question of our time doesn't differ greatly from the one which affected the Christian peoples of the Middle Ages. In a foolish way it is said to arise from hatred towards the Jewish tribe. Mosaism in itself couldn't become an object of hate for Christians, since, until the coming of Christ, it was the only true religion, a prefiguration of and preparation for Christianity, which, according to God's Will, was to be its successor. But the Judaism of the centuries [after Christ] turned its back on the Mosaic law, replacing it with the *Talmud*[ii], the very quintessence of that Pharisaism which in so many ways has been shattered through its rejection by Christ, the Messiah and Redeemer. And although Talmudism is an important element of the Jewish question, it cannot be said, strictly speaking, to give that question a religious character, because what the Christian nations despise in Talmudism is not so much its virtually non-existent theological element, but rather, its morals, which are at variance with the most elementary principles of natural ethics.

Nor does the question originate in aversion for a race, as apparently expressed by the improper adjective *Semitic* that is attached to it. In the first

[1]. Here, a list of the main works, published, in the past few years, especially in France: *La France Juive* [Jewish France], 2 vols; *La fin d'un monde* [The End of a World]; *La dernière bataille* [The Last Battle], by Edouard Drumont, Marpon and Denta, Paris; *Le juif* [The Jew], by G. des Mousseaux, Watelier, *Études historiques* [Historical Studies], by Van der Haeghen, Palmé; *L'entrée des Israélites dans la société française* [The Entry of the Israelites into French Society], Lecoffre; *Les juifs nos maîtres* [The Jews, Our Masters], by Abbé Chabautey; *Rome et les juifs* [Rome and the Jews], by Lémann; *La question juive* [The Jewish Question], by Rev. Fr. Ratisbonne, Douniol; *Les juifs, rois de l'époque* [The Jews, Kings of the Epoch], by Toussenel, 2 volumes, Marpon; *La France n'est pas juive* [France Is Not Jewish], by Reynaud, Marpon; *Le juif* [The Jew], by Kraszewki, Dentu; *Pauvre Moschko* [Poor Moschko], by Franzos, Floro; *Il sangue christiano nei riti ebraici della moderna Sinagoga* [Christian Blood in the Hebraic Rites of the Modern Synagogue], Prato, Toscana, Giachetti & Co.; *La juiverie* [Jewry], by G. de Pascal, Blériot; *La piaga ebrea* [The Hebraic Plague], by Dr. Giov. De Stampa, Treviso; *Le juif, voilà l'ennemi* [The Jew: Here's the Enemy], by Martinez, Savine; *La preponderance juive* [The Jewish Preponderance], by Abbé Joseph Lémann, Lecoffre; *La politique israélite* [Israelite Politics], by Kimon, Savine; *Socialismo, discussioni* [Socialism: Discussions], by Dr. Don Sebastiano Nicotra, Rome, Tip. Della Pace; *La Haute Banque et les Révolutions* [The High Finance and the Revolutions], by Auguste Chirac, Savine; *La Russie juive* [Jewish Russia], by Kalixt Wolski, Savine; *L'Algérie juive* [Jewish Algeria], by Georges Meynié, Savine; *Le mystère du sang chez les juifs* [The Mystery of Blood Among the Jews], by Desportes, Savine. We would like to suggest to that Italian writer who wishes to render a great service to Italy that he choose, among these and other similar ones, the above mentioned fine volume of Dr. Martinez *Le Juif, voilà l'ennemi, appel aux catholiques* [The Jew: Here's the Enemy. An Appeal to Catholics], for it contains the essence of what the most recent and most famous authors set forth, and it argues with rare logic and doctrine. If it is amplified with notes that are useful for Italy, we are convinced that it will have a wide circulation and will be a very great help in opening the eyes for the revolution that is undermining, subverting and perturbing our unfortunate peninsula. Thus we urge that this brave Italian stand up and courageously set out on the sacred work. *Fiat lux!* [Let there be light!]

place, the Israelite tribe is not the only one in the world springing from Sem's most noble blood. Nor can any reason be found why the Aryans, who derive from Japheth, should harbor an inherited hatred for Sem's offspring, in whose tabernacles, according to Noe's solemn prophecy,[iii] they even were to live in fraternal harmony. Thus we take the designation *Semitic* whenever applied to the Jewish question, and *Semitism*, whenever applied to Judaism, to be inappropriate because in exceeding the scope of their meaning, substituting the whole for a part, they produce a false [if not inflammatory] concept.

Nevertheless, aversion to the tribe adds to it and constitutes one of the chapters of the question, the religious codex of the *Talmud* being another one. Moreover, the Jewish race, in as far as it is a nation, though as such without a fixed fatherland and without a political organism, lives dispersed among the nations, perhaps not without getting mixed with them here and there, but keeping aloof from them in all things which might develop into social union, and regarding them as enemies or even as victims fallen to its greediness. Thus it is that the great Israelite family, dispersed among the peoples of the world, forms a *foreign* nation within the nations in which it resides, and the sworn *enemy* of their prosperity, since the cardinal point of Talmudism is the oppression and spoliation of the very peoples who extend hospitality to its disciples. Because of which St. Paul, at the end of his days, characterized the Jews as displeasing God and hostile to all men: *Deo non placent, et omnibus hominibus adversantur.* [Who (killed both the Lord Jesus and the prophets, and have persecuted us) please not God and are adversaries to all men.][2]

And that the sinister codex of the *Talmud*, even beyond the rules of an execrable morality, commands hatred of all men who don't have Jewish blood, and especially Christians, and makes it licit to spoliate and ill-treat them like noxious beasts, isn't any longer one of its doctrinal points that can be denied. It is not the work of Rohling, whom we too acknowledge to be a writer who in part indulges in fancies and invents arbitrary quotations, but the most careful and most serious study of the *Mishna*, which is the *Talmud's* text, and the *Gemara*, which is its annotation, besides the study of several rabbis, including the most notable ones of past and present times,[iv] that does away with any doubt whatsoever. It would be enough to consult the work of Achille Laurent, which the Hebrews have taken nearly out of circulation because it masterfully reveals the secrets of Talmudism regarding the extermination of Christian civilization and which is thus able to persuade even the most unwilling and the most doubtful.[3] We have, for the rest, adduced incontestable proof of that already in the past, which to repeat would be superfluous here.

---

[2]. I Thess. 2:18.
[3]. *Rélation des affaires de Syrie* [Report of the Affairs of Syria], Paris, 1846.

Besides it will be of use to refer to two documents which very clearly establish the true condition of the Israelites in the countries extending them refuge, as well as the main reason for the problems they create there, and thus for the aversion they incur there. The first one stems from the famous legal consultant Portalis, written at the beginning of this century, when Napoleon I intended to legally acknowledge full civil equality of the Jews with the French. The erudite man who drew up a respective memorandum, of which the day will still come when *meminisse iuvabit* [it will help to remember], observed that the question being the Hebrews, religious tolerance towards them didn't need to be confused with granting them civil status. He said:

> For the Jews are not simply a *sect*, but a *people*. This people, who in antiquity had their own land and government, were dispersed, but not destroyed: they roam about the earth in order to look for a refuge, but not a homeland; they are to be found within all the nations but meld with none of them; they settle as strangers in a strange land. This is due to the nature of Jewish institutions. As conquest was the very goal of Rome's power, war the goal of the republic of Sparta, culture the goal of the state of Athens, commerce the goal of the dominion of the Carthaginians, so *religion* is that of the Hebraic tribe for whom religion is everything, the basis and law of its society. Hence follows the evident fact that the Jews everywhere form a nation within a nation; and although they live in France, in Germany, in England, they never become French, German, or English. Rather, they remain Jews and nothing but Jews.

A truth later being harshly confirmed by Crémieux, the great vassal of the reigning Judaism, and by the Jewish review *L'Alliance israélite*, that defined the Hebrew as *the man of an inexorable universalism*. Whence Portalis concludes aptly that it is perfectly in accord with justice that this kind of foreign body, which, by virtue of its institutions, its principles, and its customs, yet always remains aloof from the common society, would remain subject to laws of exception.

The other document is the manifesto of thirty-one members of the legislative chamber of Romania, addressed to the powers who, in 1868, arrogated to impose to their state the law of civil equality of the Hebrews. In substance these members of parliament say,

> The Jews, obedient to necessity, ostensibly comply with the authority of the non-Jewish state; but they are never able to consent to become an integral part of it, because they are unable to shed the idea of their own state. They not only form a religious sect, but also a complex of indelible uniqueness of birth and of resolute belief in an

Part I ~ The Causes

always exclusively Jewish nationality, which all of them without exception maintain amidst other peoples. Because of this, it is impossible for them to unite in blood with other peoples, and impossible to partake with them their sentiments, which are directly opposed in all things to those of Christians. And the biggest obstacle lies in religion, which is their religious and civil law alike, thus constituting the political and social cult and organism. Hence Judaism, wherever it gains a footing, necessarily establishes a state within a state.

Concerning gratitude towards the peoples who shelter them, the Israelites regard themselves as absolved, since they believe them to be usurpers. Just to the contrary, they use every sort of means in order to gain supremacy over them, of which they believe to have been assured by the *Old Testament*. The time they pass within the bosom of other people is for them, so to speak, a time of penance, punishment and exile; and the inhabitants of the countries harboring them pass for enemies which, as soon as the promised hour of universal Jewish dominion over the world will have come, are to be subjugated.

The corollary of this situation is that the Jew nowhere has his fatherland, i.e., the land of his fathers, and therefore that corollary is the *patriotism* of which he permanently boasts and for whose apostle he passes himself off, but only in order to reach his goal of ruining and devouring the nations which have accorded him the right of citizenship. A bold imposture. That is also the reason why the most hateful trade of being a traitor and spy is one of their characteristics. Well known is Bismarck's dictum: "God created the Hebrew in order to serve the man who needs him as a spy," and the other one of Count Cavour, who used to say of a certain Hebrew, his confidant:

> He is most useful to me, in order to let the public know what I wish it to know. The very moment I have finished speaking with him he has already betrayed me.

In July, the *Kreuz-Zeitung* [Journal of the Cross] of Berlin published this account of an army officer:

> During the 1870 war, I was assigned to the 10th Corps, commanded by General Voigts-Rhetz. He was granted 100,000 thalers to pay spies. He returned to Berlin, that sum not having been touched, because he hadn't succeeded in recruiting any Frenchmen. However, in 1866, in the war against Austria, things went differently: the Jews showed up in great numbers and sold us for a small price all news concerning the movements of the imperial army; these Jews were Austrian citizens and so, voluntary spies.

The Jewish Question in Europe

History is replete with treason committed by Hebrews to the detriment of the state as well as of public or private persons. A few years ago the Jew Goldsmit stole and sold the top secret documents of the Great-Prussian state. The Jew Klotz betrayed the English general Hicks and his troops, who then were killed by the Mahdi's barbarians in the Sudan. The Jew Adler abused the trust Krajewski had put in him and handed him over to the Prussians. The Jew Deutz betrayed the Duchess of Berry for 500,000 francs. And so has it been already in past centuries, beginning with the Jew Sedecia, who poisoned Charles the Callow, up to the Jewess Païva, who of late was busy to acquire the battle plans of the French army in Paris, in order to sell them.

The other element making the organism of the Hebrews in the Christian countries extremely dangerous and multiplying a hundred-fold the abhorrence of them there is the superstition taken from the *Talmud* which holds that the Israelites not only form the *highest race* of mankind, which is totally comprised of races inferior to them, but also are solely, by full divine right, entitled to the possession of the entire universe, which they will one day enjoy. Because of this insane belief, Judaism has insinuated itself everywhere; moreover it can be said to be the central dogma of what the Jews call their religion. Therein lies the depraved doctrine of messianism that they profess from the third century of the Christian era, when the Babylonian *Talmud* was compiled, until today, and whoever, following the course of time, traces the commentaries of the greatest rabbis, will find it to be unwavering and always identical, as in our time is revealed by the Jew Disraeli, who became Lord Beaconsfield and head of Great Britain's government. He, who assumed the Anglican color in order to rise to power, wrote in his famous book, *Coningsby*:

> No penal law, no physical torment will ever cause a *superior race* to be devoured by an *inferior race*. The bastardized and persecuting one (our Christian one) disappears, but the pure-bred and persecuted one (the Jewish one) reigns and endures. It is thus in vain that they rush upon us Jews, contaminating and humiliating us, while they dissolve through centuries and decades of centuries: the Jew's soul rises up and takes up its way again, getting ahead, and in our days already exercises an influence over Europe's affairs that is thoroughly miraculous.

He added this after having assured that "the modern world is governed by persons far different than is imagined by those who cannot see what is going on behind the scenes"; and by this he intended to say that the Jews manipulate everything from the shadows.

Part I ~ The Causes

If it were necessary we could accumulate proofs of this proud belief, culling them throughout the centuries. But doing so would be superfluous. The falsification of the prophetic tradition regarding the Messiah and His kingdom among the people, which is the Church, already began with the destruction of Jerusalem and the dispersion or enslavement of the Jewish people by the victorious Romans. Suetonius handed down its memory in his *Lives of the 12 Caesars*: *Percrebuerat Oriente toto vetus et constans opinio, esse in fatis, ut eo tempore Judei profecti rerum potirentur.* [In the entire East had spread the old and consistent opinion that it had been prophesied that at that time the Jews would come forth and would possess the power.] And, in his historiography, Tacitus corroborated this: *Pluribus persuasio inerat, antiquis sacerdotum literis contineri eo ipso tempore fore ut valesceret Oriens, profectique Judei rerum potirentur.* [Many held the opinion that it was contained in the ancient writings of the priests that this was the time when the East would become strong and the Jews would come forth and possess the power.] Similarly speaks St. Jerome, who was most competent as to the true and false opinions of the Jews.

Drach, a convert to Christianity and a profound expert on the *Talmud* and the Jewish mysteries, explains the doctrine of the ancient and modern teachers of Israel as follows:

> The Messiah has to be a great conqueror who puts the nations under the yoke of the Jews. They will anew take possession of the Holy Land, victorious and loaded with the riches taken from the infidels. The purpose of the coming of the Messiah will be to liberate the dispersed Israel, leading it back into the Holy Land and establishing a temporal kingdom there that is to last until the end of the world. Then all peoples will be subject to the Jews, who will treat the persons and their goods at their discretion. The scholars and rabbis of the Synagogue routinely end their discourse by invoking this triumph and all of the blessings which they expect from the coming of a Messiah of such a nature. But one of these blessings is the greatly desired moment of the slaughter of the Christians and of the complete extermination of the Nazarene's sect.[4]

The same concept, although slightly changed, is cherished by these modernized Jews who no longer give great weight to the rancid legends of the *Talmud*. The actual Messiah is replaced by a *messianic people*,[v] *i.e.*, the Israelites, predestined (but they don't know how or why) to rule over all mankind. Such a concept, among others of recent times, comes from Crémieux, the apostle of such a concept and a main founder of current Jewish power, who commented on it:

---

[4]. *L'Église et la Synagogue* [The Church and the Synagogue], pages 18, 19.

Israel will never have an end. Its little family is the greatness of God. A messianism of the new ages will be born and unfold. A Jerusalem of a new order, sacredly situated between the East and the West, will succeed the double-faced city of the Caesars and the Popes.

Stamm, a German Hebrew, has published a book, in order to announce to the world that "the reign of universal liberty on earth will be established by the Jews"; and we have seen the beautiful liberty which these insane ones dream of for the Christians. Another one of them, native of Frankfurt, wrote already in 1858:

Rome, which 1800 years ago, laid the Jews under its feet, will have to fall in ruins through the intervention of this very same people, that by doing so, will spread its light over the universe and bring the greatest advantage to mankind.

Thus it has to be kept the same, that Judaism is always an alien and always inimical power in those countries where it takes root, but also a power tending to overwhelm and dominate the inhabitants, by virtue of its inherent dogmatic and civil, juridical and national constitutions. And Judaism does so by all sorts of evil tricks and perfidy.

What just has been said is proven by the doctrines no less than by the most evident everyday facts.

As for the doctrines, here we have some central points of the moral-religious instruction which are imposed and inculcated by the *Talmud*, the supreme codex of this entire race. The basic principle of Jewish morals in which originate the rules for practical behavior toward one's fellow man, states that other men, compared to the Hebrew, are no more than animal beasts. The *Talmud* exclaims:

O seed of Abraham, the Lord has spoken to you through Ezekiel's mouth: you are my sheepfold; that is, you are human beings, whereas the other peoples of this world are not at all humans, but beasts.[5]

The Jew who rapes and kills a non-Jewish woman must be absolved in court, because he has done evil to "a mare."[6] Maimonides, who is considered infallible in the ghettos, states in his treatise on homicide that the Israelite who kills a *goy*[vi] or a non-Jewish man cannot be punished. Doesn't that suffice? One of the books of Israel that has authority seriously asserts that "the non-Jews are black animals" or, in other words, wild boars.[7] And so in such a way are treated all those who aren't of its nationality by this race, that by its

---

[5]. Treatise, Bava Metzia, fol. 114.1.
[6]. Treatise, Berakhoth, fol. 88. 1.
[7]. Treatise, Salkutre-Ubeni, fol. 10, 3.

sexual excesses, was disgusting even to the Romans of the Caesars' epoch, so that Tacitus called it *proiectissima ad libidinem gens* [a people wholly addicted to debauchery].

Enough? No, for the *Talmud* elevates the Jew above all humankind; and teaches that an Israelite is more pleasing to God than the angels of paradise; that to strike a Jew is to strike God; that the non-Hebrew, he who thrashes a son of Jacob, deserves no less than death.

Another edifying chapter of Jewish morals is the one that, in the *Talmud*, concerns the oath. Three Jews sitting in judgment have the power to nullify any oath and to absolve from any promise whatsoever. Drach well explains this ceremony, which is called *Kol-Nidrei*. The *Talmud* affirms that the three judges possess the same authority as the Tribunal of Moses.[8]

Aside from this, the Hebrews have their varying external rituals and their varied formulas or paraphrases by means of which they intend to take not or to invalidate the oath, to which nevertheless they swear. This entire accumulation of malfeasances, which they and their loyalists have calumniously imputed to the Jesuits' morals, conversely is practised by themselves with unscrupulous religiosity. Better still, the night before the feast of Kippur, they absolve themselves, through certain ones of their ceremonies and contradictions, of all bonds of conscience with which they have contracted under a more formal binding force, thus fulfilling [or not fulfilling] all of their obligations of conscience, past, present, or future ones, just as it pleases them and redounds to their advantage. Moreover, according to the *Talmud*, in a case between a Christian and a Hebrew, the Jewish judge must always, as far as possible, let his fellow Jew win.

In a similar manner, this codex of morals permits, and even commands, that the Jew appropriate to himself things lost by a non-Jew. Behold the incredible reason: "Returning something to the non-Jew means to make oneself unworthy of God's mercy."[9] And, indeed, Maimonides reminds of the strict obligation of practising this trickery: "Who returns something", he wrote, "commits a sin, because he increases the power of the impious."[10]

The legitimacy of robbing Christians is impudently taught by the rabbinical schools. "Since the life of the idolaters (as Christians are considered by Jews) was left to the Israelites' discretion, their wealth is still much more left to their [the Israelites'] discretion." This is the doctrine of Rabbi Joseph Albo.[11] The possessions of Christians, according to *Bava Baria*, are—or

---

[8]. Treatise, Rosh-Hashanah, fol. 25, ff.
[9]. Treatise, Bava Kama, fol. 29, 50 and Treatise, Sanhedrin, fol. 76, 5.
[10]. In his treatise *On robbery and lost things*, cap. IX, art. 3, 4.
[11]. *Fundamentals of the Faith*, Part III, chapter 25.

ought to be—like the desert or the seashore: the first one to occupy them will be their owner, provided that this first one be an Israelite. Such is the teaching of Rabbi Pfefferkorn.[12] "It is permissible to cheat a Christian as much as possible. Usury imposed on a Christian is not only permissible but even a good work, and for this reason it is lawful to impose it on holy days also. But a Christian is so much to be plundered [by usury] that he remains ruined."[13] These rabbinical documents are considered holy.

That these flowers of Jewish morality—which contain still more turpitudes with which we don't wish to dirty our pen—don't fall on deaf ears, is known from experience by all the nations being afflicted with this race. The illustrious Maxime du Camp has already published a monograph on the Jewish thieves of Paris which would merit being translated into every language.[14] But Colonel Cerfbeer, a Jew by birth, calculated in his 1847 studies in France, the number of Jews convicted of robbery doubled, relative to the number of French convicted for the same reason, and he added this warning of inestimable value:

> What differentiates the Hebrew delinquents from the others is that their crimes are of a more malignant perversity because they are the result of premeditation. Such crimes include sponging, falsification, usury, legacy-hunting, premeditated bankruptcy, contraband, counterfeiting, fraudulent selling of hypothecated property, extortion, swindle and fraud of all sorts and with every sort of aggravating circumstances.[15]

Except that, forty years later, Talmudic ethics has made further progress, the worst of it being that, thanks to the civil equality Judaism now has in nearly all of Europe, most of the crimes committed by Jews go unpunished one way or another, and are sometimes even rewarded by knights' ribbons and crosses or baronial titles.

Thus whoever investigates the facts and documents objectively, cannot but conclude that there has never been an ambition more mad, more tenacious, and more impudently confessed than that of the Jews. They arrogate to themselves the conquest of the world, the rule over all the reigns which they will have defeated, the subjugation of all the peoples. And they ascribe themselves the right to lay claim to all of the wealth of the universe as their legitimate possessions, given them by God. Indeed, as one reads and hears about a handful of men—about 8 million—throwing this monstrous

---

[12]. *Philosophical Dissertations*, p. 11.
[13]. Shulcan Arukh, Choshen Mishpat. F. 348, n. *I jore d'cáss.* 159 n. i.
[14]. See *Revue des deux mondes* [Journal of Two Worlds], June 1, 1869.
[15]. *Les Juifs* [The Jews].

challenge in the face of the one and a half billion others and seriously boasting about one day defeating them, one imagines being in a dream!

Nevertheless, they never stop lamenting the persecutions which they underwent in the past and which they are still now undergoing here and there! But these persecutions were and are the consequence of their mad wickedness. Everywhere they paraded and parade their avid ambition; everywhere they bragged and brag about their divinely given superiority over the peoples among whom they lived and live; everywhere they showed and show themselves to be intractable, hostile and malevolent towards the nations that tolerated or tolerate them and even bestowed or bestow upon them the blessing of the right of citizenship.

A universal effect always corresponds to an equal cause. The aversion to Judaism did not only rise among Christians—because of the Jews' deicide on Calvary—but also existed and continues existing among the Mussulmen, the Arabs, the Persians, as it already prevailed with the Greeks, the Egyptians, and the Romans.

The famous P. Ratisbonne, an Israelite by birth, and through his conversion turned into a fervent servant of Christ, discussed very wisely the persecutions that arose in every age and place against his ancient fellows:

> The Jews' evil is that they don't understand to open their eyes to recognize the true causes of the persecution inflicted on them in all centuries and without peer in history. Down through the ages many people were maltreated by others. These tortures, however, came to an end and moreover didn't take place all over the world simultaneously. But the persecution of the Jews is marked by its perpetuity and its universality. Thus it is a unique case which cannot be explained in purely human terms.[16]

And because of that the author traced things back to the designs of God's justice, which, through the persecution of this people, the emulator on earth of the satanic rebellion in heaven, proves itself to be inexorable.

Nonetheless, the human causes of this fact, unique in history, are due to their insatiable appetite for enriching themselves via usury, for predomination through malice and for dominion by occupying and snatching up in the states as much as possible.

It is the immutable law of the Hebrews' prosperity in any given country that they always prosper at the expense of its inhabitants' wealth and liberty. Some years before Rome fell into the claws of the secret societies, the famous

---

[16]. *La Question juive* [The Jewish Question].

Lémann brothers, Jewish converts, became Catholic priests. In one of their works which merits deep meditation they wrote:

> O Israelites of Rome, we know the attitudes of our people. If you were given the property rights you wish, we wager that thirty, or at most, fifty years hence, Rome would no longer belong to the Catholic Christians but be in your hands.[17]

And the prophecy is about to come to pass. The city of Rome rapidly approaches the yoke which will subjugate her, materially and economically, to the Hebrews' dominion, as it already has occurred in nearly all the metropoles of the major states of Europe.

But it is just this subjugation burdening the European peoples in economic, moral and political aspects that constitutes the kernel of the Jewish question in our time.

In the last century to whose advantage has the revolution been made which has upset the entire Christian order of practically every state? Not to the advantage of the peoples that it has left oppressed; not to the advantage of the monarchies which have emerged weakened from it. Looked at more closely, it must be said that it has solely been made to the advantage of Judaism, which by virtue of the lying principles of liberty, fraternity and equality, has undisturbedly succeeded in coloring over its dark plan of obtaining the predominance—and this to an extent never before attained—a plan because of which the sword of divine wrath dispersed its adherents all over the earth. If there is any case at all where the jurists' dictum comes true—*Is fecit cui prodest* [He has done it who profits from it]—then it is here.

On June 29, 1869, a great synod of Israelites, having come together from all over Europe, took place in Leipzig, presided over by Dr. Lazarus of Berlin. Between the more rigorous Talmudists and the modernized ones, which, although being lax and imbued with rationalism, share with the others their hatred towards Christianity, lengthy disputes arose. But finally all of them unanimously approved this proposal put forward by Dr. Philipson of Bonn, and strongly supported by Astruc, the High Rabbi of Belgium:

> The synod recognizes that the development and practice of modern principles offers the most solid security for the present and future prosperity of Judaism and its followers. These principles contain the most efficacious seeds for its thriving vitality and its further expansion.

And in effect, the *modern principles,* or the so-called *rights of man,* were invented by Jews, in order to cause the people and their governments to

---

[17]. *Rome et les juifs* [Rome and the Jews].

divest themselves of their defensive arms against Judaism, and to multiply the offensive arms redounding to this latter's advantage. Once having acquired absolute civil liberty and equality in every sphere with Christians and the nations, the dam which previously had held back the Hebrews was opened for them, and in a short time, like a devastating torrent, they penetrated and cunningly took over everything: gold, trade, the stock market, the highest appointments in political administrations, in the army, and in diplomacy; public education, the press, everything fell into their hands or into the hands of those who were inevitably depending upon them. The result was that in our days Christian society encounters in the very laws and constitutions of the states the biggest obstacle which hinders it from shedding the yoke of Hebrew audacity, imposed under the guise of liberty.

This is the source of the presumption of Judaism, which, as said Prince Metternich, supplies the states with "first-class revolutionaries," and of the arrogance by which it already predicts its definitive triumph over Christianity. In Paris, Stern, a Hebrew, was able to exclaim in front of a big audience: "Within ten years, I don't know how a Christian will still be able to live." And this Croesus, who among the princes of Israel is Hirsch, watching from the top of the staircase of his regal palace the élite of the nobles of France coming up the steps for a party in his rooms, said to his son: "Do you see these people? In twenty years all of them will be either our sons-in-law or our door-keepers." And, unfortunately, he was right.

These are the summarized and epitomized causes of the Jewish question. In a further article we will demonstrate its principal effects.

PART II

THE EFFECTS

That series of assertions which in 1789 was said to be the synthesis of the *rights of man*, in fact represented nothing but the *rights of Jews*, to the detriment of the peoples in whose bosom the practice of these rights was advanced. These rights were, so to speak, the bulwark of power by means of which, in our century, Judaism laid siege to Christian society, assaulted it, upset it and, to a great extent, overtook it. This is seen in the universal stupor in which Europe finds itself as it perceives that gold, the dissemination of ideas, and the political-irreligious tendency of its states are nearly entirely in Hebrew hands. So much so that Chabany was able to truthfully print a book entitled, *Les juifs nos maîtres* [*The Jews Our Masters*], without being contradicted by anyone.

Already in 1847, Cerfbeer, the president of the Israelite Central Consistory of France, described the success of his fellow Jews in that country:

> The Jews, in proportion to their number, occupy more posts than Catholics and Protestants combined. Their ruinous influence is at work more than ever in those affairs which most of all burden the nation's patrimony. There is no business in which they do not considerably participate, no public loan which they do not hold, no disastrous crash which they have not engineered and from which they do not profit. But unjustifiably they are lamenting, almost daily. Unjustifiable because they are those who enjoy the best of the favors and gain advantage over the others.[1]

Later, the convert, P. Ratisbonne, added:

---
[1] *Les juifs* [The Jews], page 9.

The Jewish Question in Europe

> Through their dexterity and ingenuity, as well as through their lust of power, the Jews have step by step occupied every way leading to wealth, dignity and power. Their spirit, so to speak, imbues modern society. They regulate the stock exchange, the press, theater, literature, the great trade channels by land, as well as by sea, and by possessing the capitals as well as through their shrewdness, at present they hold captive, like in a net, all of Christian society.[2]

And that is occurring not only in one region of Europe, but nearly in all of them excepting Russia.[vii] As in the time of Arianism, the hour in which the Christian world, without realizing it, found itself Arian, thus today, Europe finds itself mired, and to a great extent no longer Christian, but Jewish or Judaizing. So, the question has arisen which will have to be resolved some time or other, and this according to the legal claims of Christianity.

Sebastiano Nicotra quotes the passage from an old manuscript, lately discovered, in which a Hebrew, in the following terms, discloses the key of Jewish power in our days:

> My sons, Jehovah is with us, and in his mercy he has reserved to us a powerful weapon, or better said, an invincible force, that is to raise us in the midst of the nations of Christ and to subject them to our domination. This force is named in the holy book, and it is called usury. The holy book, as you know, prohibits us from practising usury among brothers, within our own tribe and against those of our kind; but it doesn't prohibit its practice against the foreigner, the infidel, the enemy. It therefore serves us as a weapon of war and an instrument of victory. Thus, usury remains to us, and better than the faith and morals of Christ, usury is the little stone that fell from the mountain and is to cover the world; the mustard seed that is to grow into that superb tree which will dominate the world.[3]

Nine years ago, a great rabbi, speaking in Paris to his faithful, said:

> Under pretext of aiding the masses of workers, we must excessively tax the estates of the big landowners and as soon as their property [through usury] will have been transferred to us, the Christian proletarians' labour will totally fall to our advantage. 'Poverty is slavery', said a poet.
>
> The proletarians are the speculators' lowest servants, but oppression and arrogance humbly serve the cunning. And who could deny the sons of Israel's cunning, prudence and perspicacity?

---

[2] *La Question juive* [The Jewish Question], page 9.
[3] *Socialismo, discussioni* [Socialism: Discussions], page 339-340.

Part II ∽ The Effects

This essence of Talmudic doctrine has permeated the soul of contemporary Judaism, mindful of the *Bible's* words, *Pecuniae obediunt omnia* [All things obey money]. By means of freedom to practise usury, Michelet wrote,[4]

> The Jews have resolved the problem of volatizing wealth: redeemed by the bill of exchange, they are free men now, they are masters now; from one box on the ear to another, they have ascended to the throne of the world.

In March the director of the *Pall Mall Gazette* in London sent one of his correspondents to Berlin to interview the court chaplain, Stoecker, one of the most zealous leaders of the anti-Semitic league of Germany. This man declared, in substance, to the emissary from London,

> I do not hate the Jews, nor do I wish them evil through religious hatred. But as God's servant as a Lutheran pastor, and as a representative of the nation, I cannot remain quiet, since I see and feel the infinite evil that the Jews have done and still do to my country, and especially to Berlin. Here the Hebrew has all of the gold in his hand, and consequently, he also has all of the power in his hand. I don't detest the Hebrews because they are rich, but because they accumulate riches through dishonest methods. In the countryside they cheat the merchants and in the city they make dirty profits. I maintain what I have already said repeatedly: that from the viewpoints of trade, of social interests, of politics and morals, the Jews are leading Germany into the abyss.

In Germany the situation has reached such a point that in September Mr. Ahlward was able in Berlin to publish his book *The Desperate Struggle between the Aryan Peoples and Judaism*, filled with such fearful evidence that the government believed it was necessary to confiscate the book.

In this same month, as did the German parliament, so also the Austrian one resounded with loud warning cries against the falling financial predominance of Judaism.

The Jews were ten times banned from the territories of the House of Austria and eventually took firm hold there under Ferdinand I., the brother of the Emperor Charles V. There they were admitted, and they remained there in the condition of servants of the Holy Empire, up to the time of Maria Theresia, who favored them in different ways, depending on the various provinces. In the German patrimonial dominions they were forbidden entry, except in Vienna, whereas they were admitted in the reign of St. Wenceslas [= Bohemia], but on the condition that they didn't exceed a fixed number of

---

[4] See *Le Contemporain* [The Contemporary], July 1, 1881

families. They were more generously tolerated in the reign of St. Stephen [= Hungary], nevertheless leaving them forbidden entry or immigration from other regions. The maximum of liberty they enjoyed uniquely in Trieste. From the ghettos of the Duchy of Mantua, from the Republic of Venice, from the Papal States and from the Levant, they were allowed to come into our area of Trieste, because of which today they feign, under the cloak of *patriotism*, such a remarkable devotion to Trieste. After the first detachment from Poland had arrived, also the Jews of Galicia and other Polish regions gained the same privileges of Trieste. Finally, from 1848 to 1869, all of the defensive restrictions of the Empire were repealed, and Judaism was free to occupy it and to make itself its master, which indeed it has done, and continues to do at present.[viii]

During the Viennese Reichsrat's discussion regarding the Jewish question, the valiant orator, Lueger, had to say, amid the approval of the majority of deputies:

> Is the universal domination of the Hebrews only a fairy tale? Look at France, look at Hungary. In this latter country, the basest of the Hebrews has more power than even the Cardinal Primate. And aren't here in Austria the concerns of the Northern Railway, and those of petrol, and those of coal—all of this having been ceded to the Hebrews to their advantage—proofs of the predominance of Jews? And is not a serious argument in favor of their predominance that the president of the Reichsrat intends to ask our colleague, Pattaï, not to speak here of Rothschild, for fear that he might cut down the exchange of our public funding?

Once more we must cite the example of Austria-Hungary, so corrupted by Judaism, worse than a vineyard fallen prey to phylloxera [vastatrix].[ix] At present this renewed indication is suitable.

The progeny of Abraham, in ten years, has increased by 2.07 per cent [*sic!*—but evidently this erroneous number must be corrected into 43 per cent] there: from 1,154,000 descendants of Abraham in 1869 to 1,648,708 today. After 1848 in Hungary, and after 1862 in the rest of the Empire, the Jews extorted the legal authorization to possess their own land. In such a brief interval, the Rothschild family, in Bohemia alone, acquired a quarter of the land, which was in the possession of the sixty oldest homes in the realm; and now they alone possess seven times more than the imperial family. Today, in the realm of St. Stephen, the Jews have such a great power that they enjoy more than a quarter of the electoral votes which, in the elections, are reserved for the big landowners; and at present they begin to decorate themselves with the titles and the names of the most illustrious lineages of that region. Half of the County of Neutra now belongs to a single Hebrew, Baron Poppel.

The Hungarian public debt, which in 1873 was 221 million, rose in 1885 to 1461 million, and now is more than 1600 million. And the minister, Tisza, the great patron of the Jews, three years ago proposed giving a seat of honor in the court to Alberto Rothschild and his wife, in recognition of his merits in sponging off the national credit. To accord him this is to add to the mockery.

But even more devastated is Galicia. The Jews, in a little more than twenty years, have assumed ownership of 80 percent of its territory, and continue always to buy up those country seats and estates which are put up for auction because of unpaid taxes.

The arrogance of this race in the Hapsburg Empire has come to such, that not long ago a Viennese Jewish alderman publicly responded to a Christian alderman who was complaining of the too firm footing the Jews were gaining everywhere:

> If the Christians are unable to tolerate this state of affairs, there is a quick remedy: let them leave the Empire, let them emigrate as they please.

Things won't go on this way much longer, and two million foreign usurers will have robbed of their entire patrimony the 40 million Austro-Hungarians who granted them hospitality and civil equality, and throughout the Empire will revive the custom that flocks of slaves cultivate the farms, to the pure profit of the new masters. The old princes' and magnates' descendants will hoe the vegetable gardens and the fields of the emancipated rag dealers of Vienna, Presburg and Buda; and sons of the former owners will wash the feet of the Sarahs and Judiths.

We could also cite the example of the Balkans, especially that of Romania, upon which the 1878 Congress of Berlin, dominated by hidden Jewish power, imposed the obligation of equalizing the Hebrews in all respects to their fellow countrymen and fellow citizens; and at present, they are undisturbedly devouring this kingdom like insatiable grasshoppers. We could cite Russia, where the land owned by the nobility is more than two-thirds mortgaged to German bankers, who are mostly Jews, and where, day by day, the land of the farmers is falling more into the hands of the Kulaks, that is, of the usurers. But let us cast a glance at our Italy, where for thirty years Judaism lords it and plunders, just as if Italians were its loot conquered from enemies.

The approximately fifty thousand Jews who make themselves at home on the Peninsula have their headquarters there in Venice, in the territory of Mantua, in the ancient Extended States, and in the territory of Ferrara. In this region, which can be called the *Italian Judea*, they are the superintendents in all things and over all things. There is almost not a single lira spent without their approval. Retail trade, industry, currency exchange, wholesale, rural and urban real estate depend on them. Suffice it to say that four-fifths of the provincial territory of Padua is owned by the Hebrews and that, with the mortgage in their hand, they control disposal of the remaining fifth. Ancona, Livorno and Florence live under the usurious yoke of the Israelites. Some of these already look forward to the day when the most sumptuous villas, the biggest land holdings and the most famous patrician palaces will come under their ownership, in order to serve as collateral for the loans granted by them to the careless or silly owners who are unable to free themselves from them. Two years ago one of these Hebrews who perhaps not long ago had lived from hand to mouth selling matches in the Florentine promenades of the Arno river, died leaving to his sons the trifle of 18 million in cash, amassed as God only knows.

We prefer to say nothing of Rome. More than by the Italian bayonets, it is seized by the nooses of the great Jewish net, which detains all sorts of little and big fish therein; these nevertheless remain swallowed up in a succession of troubles, weeping, and misery, moving one to pity. Usury, which in this capitol is practised by Judaism far more than by Italians, reigns supreme there, and along with usury pompously go arm-in-arm fraud, graft, and plunder. And whoever would penetrate into the mysteries of that pell-mell formed by the public works, the public monopolies and the various companies that serve the state, would see with horror the millions being swallowed up with that same impudence with which the Grand Master of Italian Masonry, through the public tobacco supply, has earned his merits. In August 1887 a Jew wrote these noteworthy words from Rome to a German Jewish newspaper:

> The honorable Francesco Crispi [a 33rd degree Mason and Grand Master of the Italian Grand Orient] is the best friend of the Hebrews and protects their interests with all his soul. In this way, we Jews have a great influence in the government in Italy; this gives us much pleasure, because we may hope to make good profits and to enjoy the fruit of our labor, without being bothered.[5]

More than every other country, France merits to be considered under this point of view. Drumont's revelation, clarifying the accumulation of money by the Hebrews under the aegis of the *rights of man*—the system initiated a hundred years earlier and also in France—is ample cause for loathing. Let us follow up on this. In 1791 the Jews there were only a few thousand;

---

[5] *Jüdische Presse* [Jewish Press], August 8, 1887.

Part II ⁓ The Effects

they had been banned by the king many times, since being an evil plague on the nation. Now they might surpass 60,000, and they approach 100,000, altogether with an appearance, with a language, with names proving them to stem from Frankfurt, Hamburg, Poland, Portugal. The bloody revolution of 1793 which wasted the goods of the nobility and the clergy, attracted that swarm of rapacious vultures. A century later here in France, perhaps even more so than in the Austrian Empire and in Italy, they have become the lords of everything.

If one relies upon the recent calculation, the Hebrews, who are the masters of half the capital circulating in the world, possess 80 billion in France alone, while the total French capital is estimated at 150 to 200 billion! In order to get an idea of the monstrous fortune accumulated there by the Jews, it is advisable to compare their number with that of the natives. It results from this comparison that, on the average, each Jew possesses a capital of 800,000 to 1,200,000 francs, whereas in proportion, each Frenchman possesses a capital which doesn't surpass 6,000 francs. The house of Rothschild, on its own, notoriously possesses a fortune of 3 billion francs. The Prince of Bismarck affirmed that when old James, the founder of that house died, he left his beneficiaries 100 million, accumulated in about fifty years. But when he came to France, his fortune was no more than 10 million!

Everyone in Paris knows the palaces of this family of Hebrew Croesuses. These homes are estimated at 30 million, and the lavish interior equipment at another 30 million. This same sum is reached by the castles and estates in which they rejoice. Thus, there are another 120 million of properties brought to light, which this house enjoys right under the eyes of the French, who are not at all ignorant of the thousands of millions that it owns in liquid capital. But it [house of Rothschild] isn't the only one. The entire so-called *High Finance* is in the grip of non-French Jews who possess inestimable wealth. The litany of these princes of Israel is long and all have last names which sound as French as those of Arabs or Zulus. The Dreyfuses, Bichoffsheims, Oppenheims, Erlangers, Hottinguers, and so on, altogether form a banking sanhedrin that represents a value of at least 10 billion, entirely extracted from the veins of France, thanks to the *rights of man*, invented by this cosmopolitan and insatiable race itself and granted to it.

Among the 600 bankers that Paris numbers, no less than 300 have been proven to be Jews; another 100 are probably so. Moreover, they have almost totally snatched up the trades and professions of bigger and quicker profits. Half of the goldsmiths, the jewelers, the antique dealers, the furriers, the diamond-dealers, are Hebrews there. They capture and monopolize the best, with an exhibition of usury no longer knowing any restraint.

And they know ways, worse than those of usury, by means of which they have filled their safes with French gold. Innumerable are the deliberate bankruptcies, and all still remember the infamous frauds of hundreds and hundreds of millions swindled by using feigned loans and intrigues, as those of Honduras and Panama, of the *Unione generale* [General Union] of metals, and of the *Comptoir d'escompte* [Discount Bank].

In the colony of Algeria, which is bled by the Hebrews like a body in the tentacles of an octopus, by these Hebrews who, during the war of 1870, through a masterpiece of perfidy, Crémieux made legally equalize with the French and the Arabs, things don't go differently. In the newspaper, *La France*, of Paris, certainly not hostile to Judaism, Mr. Hugonnet wrote, on July 3, 1884, that this race of usurious thieves loaned soldiers one *franc*, in order to gain two the next day, which results in a rate of usury of 3,650 *francs* per 100. Maupassant, within the frame of his description of the repugnant customs of the Algerian ghettos, depicts the filthy Hebrew lying in wait of an Arab, whom he loans a silver scudo, making that man sign the obligation to pay him back four scudi in six months, or 20 in a year. If the poor man cannot do so, the greedy Jew, with his coupon in his hand, makes him sell a span of land, if he possesses that much, or the camel, or the horse, or the ragged clothes he has in his hovel. Through this subtle art, no less than all of southern Algeria has come under the power of the Israelites.

Doctor Ratzinger has legitimately observed that the expropriation of French society, by means of liquid capital, proceeds as regularly as if it were a law of nature. If nothing will be done to check its course, in fifty, or at most, in one hundred years, all of European society will be abandoned to the discretion of a handful of Jewish bankers. If these continue to enjoy the full security that they have now, by virtue of civil equality, their fortunes will continue to increase twice and threefold. If, in France alone, in the course of a century, the Jews have been able to acquire the trifle of approximately 80 billion, in another century the entire national patrimony will be in their grasp. Sixty thousand persons constitute a feudal class which will have for its servants and slaves 36 million Frenchmen. And this will be the worthy crown of the work that was begun there with the promulgation of the *rights of man*.

So as already today one cannot negotiate a loan in Europe without the good will of the Rothschilds, likewise, before long, no one will be able to do any business at all without the consent and the interest of the international Jewish league. Hebraism, with its adoration of the golden calf, which represents its power, must necessarily degrade itself below the civilized world. Exclaimed Pietro Ellero,

Part II ~ The Effects

> Now there is no longer any virtue on earth but industry, no religion other than profit, no priesthood other than business, no rite other than money-changing, no God but gold.[6]

Thus, clearly the effect of Hebrew hegemony!

The Israelite race combines the rule of gold with that one which directly subjugates the mind: we mean the magisterium of the public press and academia. In 1848, at the Jewish Congress held in Krakow and attended by the world's richest Hebrews, it was decreed that the dispersed Israel had to take possession of Europe's most powerful newspapers. "By means of this," says the statute that was approved, "the Hebrew star will spread light over the whole globe." And to satisfy oneself that this decree is effectively carried out, it suffices not just to live in the deserts of Africa.

Journalism and public education are like the two wings that carry the Israelite dragon, so that it might corrupt and plunder all over Europe. Pastor Stoecker, whom we have previously mentioned, told the messenger sent to him by the *Pall Mall Gazette* of London:

> The Jews buy the press, for half of the newspapers are in their power, and they use it on behalf of their ideas.

Already before, in the Berlin parliament, he had denounced the Jewish influence over the schools, because it is the wellspring of indescribable depravity.[x] The recent German press let us know that out of 1000 students who are enrolled in higher studies in Germany, 830 are Israelites.

In the Viennese parliament, deputy Lueger, in March of this year, told his colleagues:

> Remember, Sirs, that our schools are in the hands of the Hebrews, that our Christian teachers are suddenly put on trial, as soon as the slightest accusation against them has been made by the Hebrews; that our officials are unable to make themselves known as Christians if they want to evade persecution; that our Christian newspapers are continually confiscated.

He could have added that the Empire's universities are running over with Jewish teachers and that especially in the *Catholic* university of Vienna, there are no baptized professors, except those in the theology department. All of the others, without exception, as far as we know, are circumcised. At present even its Rector Magnificus is Jewish. What else? When it was the question of choosing a teacher for the unfortunate Archduke and successor to the throne, Rudolf, they thought they were unable to find a better one than the

---

[6]   *Questione sociale* [The social question].

Hebrew journalist, Weil, who then, under the name of Knight of Weilen, declared his conversion to Christianity, and who contributed so much to the destruction of the formerly so pious and innocent mind of the young and most unfortunate prince.

Things are going on similarly in Italy. One can truthfully say that almost all of liberal journalism of every type is directly or indirectly manipulated by Jews. Milan, Turin, Venice, Modena, Bologna and Florence live by public opinion that is being fabricated in the ghettos and in the synagogues. The so-called officious newspapers are altogether, or nearly altogether, Jewish goods sold to the government. Let us not speak of Rome, where is barely to be found a liberally behaving daily newspaper that doesn't depend on Israel. The most widely read ones, such as *La Riforma, La Tribuna, L'Opinione, Il Diritto, Il Messaggero, La Capitale, Il Capitan Fracassa*, all derive from the minds of the sons of Jacob.

But what to say about public education? We are surrounded by Hebrews in the universities, by Hebrews in the lycées, by Hebrews in the secondary schools, by Hebrews in the elementary schools. Suffice it to say that in 1885, all in all, a quarter of the students in our universities were Jews.

Let us not speak of France. In general, all of the republican newspapers which are printed there stem from Jewish hotbeds. The synopsis and catalogue of this has been exposed by Drumont and they border on the incredible. But what is worse, entirely Jewish is the pornographic and irreligious press which sullies the country and has no equal in any civilized place. And as Judaism has control of the daily newspapers and books there, thus it has control of education also, in such a way that the majority of the texts being imposed on the elementary schools have been compiled by Hebrews.[xi]

To summarize, wherever in European christendom there are Jews who enjoy civil equality, journalism, press and education either are subject to their monopoly or have to suffer under the pernicious influences of their anti-Christian bent.

But these are only the means, being destined to the end of effectively predominating over the public affairs of the states and to lead them to the ends intended by the Jews. That's the reason why they, with singular shrewdness, have made use of the rights of equality in order to occupy judicial affairs, the army, the parliament, and the cabinet councils, just as they have done in order to dominate the schools. It can be said that the Austrian empire is governed, in part secretly and in part openly, by the Hebrews; and when history will be free to give everyone his due, it will demonstrate that Austria's great military disasters in Magenta, in Solferino, and in Sadova, were owing

Part II ～ The Effects

more to treason by the Jews than to the strength of French and German strategies and weapons.

It is superfluous to speak of Italy: since 1859 it has become a reign of the Hebrews, who well know how to cheat the multitude of fools, passing themselves off as the most fervent *patriots* of the peninsula. Exclaims the valiant Dr. Giovanni de Stampa:

> What a misfortune for Italy, a nation that is proud of its strength and freedom, to have a parliament that resembles a synagogue! Italy numbers 30 million inhabitants, of which only 50,000 are Jews. Consequently, in parliament, there should be, at most, but half a Hebrew; yet instead of this they are to be found there in an alarmingly great number. Venice has the honor of being represented in parliament almost completely by Jews.[7]

But as they lord it in the chamber, so they do likewise as dignitaries in the public offices, in the banks, in the ministries, and even in diplomacy. You can't go anywhere without running into a Jewish inspector, commission president, judge, secretary or alderman. This is to say nothing regarding the municipalities, where in many places the Jews exercise despotic authority. And haven't we seen Rome being subordinated, in the most jealously guarded areas, to Hebrews who didn't even have Italian last names or, if they did have one, had borrowed it from one of our cities? Further, who might wish to call to mind the names of Italy's hundred cities needs only to observe, while taking a walk, the show-cases of the shops in the most crowded avenues of Rome, or let him survey just the lists of the heads of departments of the municipality.

The same can be said of France. In the senate and in the chamber of Paris they number more than 20; and nevertheless, their fellow-Jews are estimated at only a few more than 60,000. If the Christians were represented at this rate there, parliament would have to count no less than 40,000 senators and deputies of theirs. A few years ago 42 departments were governed by Jewish prefects, and among prefects, sub-prefects, and general receivers, there were about 200 Jews altogether.

The revolution of September 4, 1870 raised six Israelites to the apex of power; and the terrible government of the Paris Commune numbered another nine of theirs, mainly leaders and intriguers. Prominent among these were: Gustave Dacosta, who hunted the priests; Lisbonne, who tried to open a tavern served by prostitutes in nuns' habits; and, Simone Mayer, who presided over the destruction of the Vendôme column [= Napoleon's column in Paris]. Afterwards, the republic having been established, there was

---

[7] *La piaga ebrea* [The Hebraic Plague], page 17..

constituted practically no body of ministers without the participation of a Crémieux, or a Raynal, or a Magnin, or a Lockroy, or at least a Say, a Ferry, a Floquet, all husbands of women originating in Judaism.

But these bigwigs, in the same way as they do in Italy, in Austria-Hungary and in Germany, regulate the financial and political affairs according to their wishes, that is to say, on behalf of their interests and their power; in doing so, they are supported by a journalism that confuses, screens, deceives and frightens off whoever doesn't bow to the whims of Judaism. That's the reason why the cry: "The Jews are the bosses, they crush us under their feet, they reduce us to nothing." The more it is justified by the facts the more universally it spreads.

But the crowning achievement, which, with the help of the masonic sects, has increased modern Jewish power a hundredfold, is the *Universal Israelitic Alliance*, founded in Paris by Crémieux; it extends all over the globe, conferring on the various groups of Hebrews scattered to the four winds the vigor of the entire body of Israel. Its founder was therefore correct in calling it "the most beautiful and fertile institution that has ever been created in modern times, and an instrument of domination so powerful that it governs the world." In fact, it constitutes a type of executive power, of official representation of the Hebraic nation, which has the right to speak in its name.

Its organization is simple. Each Jew can take part in it, on the condition that he pays a tax of ten francs per year. It is ruled by a sanhedrin that has sixty members, bears the title of a *Central Committee*, resides in Paris, and communicates with the local committees. These leading members are elected by universal suffrage and remain in power for nine years, with a third of them replaced every three years. Wherever exist ten members, a local committee may be formed, and wherever exist several such committees, a regional committee may be set up. There is a relation of interdependence between these committees, as often as issues are in question which concern the entire association. The number of members, or adepts, surpasses 30,000, with a capital in its cash that is said to come to a million, but there is no fixed number, for the organization's Croesuses don't withhold donations to it.

Clustered around this center are numerous other societies dispersed throughout the countries; and besides the journalism, more spread across Europe, which obeys the *Alliance's* insinuation, it manages enough other journals which are printed especially for the Hebrews.

Crémieux defines its cosmopolitanism in these words:

> The *Alliance* is neither French, nor German, nor English; it is Jewish, and it is universal. This universality is exactly the reason for its prosperity and for the felicitous success it achieves.

Part II ⁓ The Effects

Whoever is desirous of forming an idea of what this *Alliance* is, can get it, in a certain way, out of the infamous novel *The Wandering Jew*, written by Eugenio Sue against the *Society of Jesus*. Whatever is calumnious with regard to the Jesuits therein, is truly historical with regard to the members of this *Alliance*. Even the Hebrews showed themselves astonished at such a comparison.

In the general assembly of February 3, 1870, one of their spokesmen answered Sue's comparison between this organization and the *Society of Jesus*:

> The comparison between the two societies is admissible regarding the extension of our contacts with the whole world, but it doesn't reach beyond that. Too enormous is the difference that, for the rest, prevails between both of them! One [that of Jesus] has the power to oppress; the other (that of Jewry) has the power to liberate; one extends in order to suffocate freedom, the other does so in order to bring it; one intends to extinguish the light, the other intends to kindle it again; one spreads the coldness of death, the other spreads the warmth of life.

It is always anew the customary language of Satan, their father (*vos ex patre diabolo estis*) [you are of your father, the devil (*John 8:44*)], who from the very first called the lie truth and death life.

From this it is not difficult to understand that a weight on the balance of the various states should be the confluence of an army of this type, consisting of men without a fatherland who pledge obedience to the commands which come out of a single center. That force became obvious when this organization, fearlessly and on equal terms, negotiated with the powers, sending diplomatic notes, protests and ultimata in order to obtain liberty for the Israelites in Romania.

Moreover, it is no mistake to consider the *Israelitic Alliance* the nerve center of Freemasonry and the uniting bond between the lodges which cover the civilized world with a net.

We are not going to assert, as various other authors do, that the sect of Freemasonry was, in its first instance, created by Jews. This assertion is not provable, and it contradicts the most circumspect examination of history. Nevertheless, it is certain that in the past century, Judaism didn't shrink from interfering in it, nor using its customary diabolical finesse from imbuing it with its spirit, directing it towards its goals, uniting itself with it, and making itself its mainspring, in order to rise as high as was not to be hoped even in a dream.

In order to arrive at this apex of domination, which was always and still is the superstitious goal of Judaism, the Israelite rabble understood quite well that there was a formidable obstacle in its way, barring its access to the baptized world, and consequently making it impossible to gain the desired dominion. We mean the Christian religion, the basis of all of the institutions and laws from which for centuries had proceeded the regulation of civil order. But in order to set about suppressing the Christian religion, and especially Catholicism, the Hebrews had to work underground, secretly sending forward others while hiding behind them, and they didn't dare to let be seen the universally detested Jewish claws. In short, they had to make their assault through foreign troops, and to bring the fort to ruin in the name of *liberty*. Thus, it was necessary to undermine this granite pedestal and the entire edifice of Christianity. And they have set to work upon this venture by placing themselves at the head of the occult world through Masonry, which is subject to them.

Meanwhile, the bonds uniting modern Judaism to Freemasonry have become so evident that it would be naïve to doubt them. Careful study of the so-called Semitic question in France, in Germany, in Italy, and elsewhere, has brought to light mysteries formerly believed to be inscrutable. Today it is known how much of its own ideas the talmudic *Cabbala* has introduced into the rites, the mysteries, the symbols, and the allegories of the masonic degrees. It is known that the Jews not only intermingle with all of the lodges and, where they are particularly numerous, fill them with members of their kind, but moreover constitute several supreme lodges or those directing all the others, to which have access only such people who are of Israelite blood and religion. Thus it is thought to be sure and perfectly certain that the entire structure of Masonry is controlled by a Hebrew sanhedrin whose power has no other limits than those of the infamous sect. Because of which one of France's most respected periodicals has justly written that

> Today, Judaism and Masonry apparently can be reduced to an identical formula: since Judaism governs the world, one has necessarily to conclude that either Masonry has become Jewish, or Judaism has become masonic.[8]

Among the recent authors whose books have come under our eyes, none who has additionally made use of the documents and arguments of others, has better demonstrated this intimate connection than the illustrious Dr. Martinez in his already quoted work, and it would be a great benefit to Italy if it were translated in due manner.[9] Thus we refer to his volume, and also to those of Drumont, of Stolz, of des Mousseaux, and of other such authors, whoever wants to become profoundly acquainted with such matters. And

---

[8]   *Revue des questions historiques* [Review of Historical Questions], April 1, 1882.
[9]   *Le juif, voilà l'ennemi* [The Jew, Here's the Enemy], 1 volume, Paris, Albert Savine, rue des Pyramides 12.

Part II ~ The Effects

meanwhile, we will conclude our enumeration of the effects proceeding from the Jewish question in Europe, indicating the practical identity which exists between the formula of Judaism and that of Freemasonry.

All that is Judaism is comprised of a love and a hate: the insatiable love of gold, *auri sacra fames*, and the inextinguishable hatred of Christ. The love serves the hate, and the hatred as well as the love are to lead to the apogée of that power, which is the Satanic delirium of reprobate Israel. Let the history of masonry be examined and it will be found that, from the past century until our days, it has intended nothing but accumulating riches and fighting to the death in Christian society, Christ and His Church. All of the predominance, overt and covert, of Freemasonry has to serve the furious Jewish eager for felling the Christian power, in order to build upon its ashes. From May 1, 1789, the day when the *rights of man* were glorified purely on behalf of the Jews, until September 20, 1870, when Rome was conquered with shells and the Papacy made a prisoner, the conspiracies, the uproars, the rebellions, the assassinations, the massacres, the wars, the so-called *revolutionary* deeds, everywhere and always had the same success of increasing the Hebrews' wealth and of humiliating and oppressing the Christian civilization. The cries "Hail!" and "Down!" varied according to prevailing need, but they were lies altogether, be it in order to fool the peoples or to palliate the misdeeds. Freedom, which in dishonor of the true God and his Christ, they pretended to raise to the throne, uniquely redounded to the Hebrews' advantage. Through it, they have acquired complete power to subjugate the nations and to ordain that the few might tyrannize the many, and this under the guise of legality, with regard to material goods, to conscience, to faith, to family, yes, and what is more, to blood and life. Out of such a spasm of liberty, equality and fraternity has arisen the despotism of the tyrannical oligarchies to which the modern states reduce themselves, and whoever glances into them will observe that they are oligarchies of Jews or of Freemasons, the Jews' base serfs. The religious right of Catholics is chained; this is the freedom of masonic Judaism. Permission of blaspheming and committing sacrileges is converted into a public right; this is its equality. Brutal hatred against whoever professes faithfulness to the God of his forefathers is applauded as patriotism; this is its fraternity. In the Rome of the Popes, carrying the Cross of Christ through the streets in a procession is a crime; but carrying the bust of Giordano Bruno or the horns of Satan there is a noble homage paid to the state. Thus, in practice, so it is that Judaism and Masonry intermingle and become a unity, like the sword with the hand of the murderer that wields it, or like the torch with the hand of the arsonist who clutches it.

The Jewish Question in Europe

Everywhere the Hebrews have stuffed, fattened, and enriched themselves by the blood of the peoples and the Church; but the Masons have not at all been left empty-handed. Look at Italy. As the Hebrews, so Freemasons too find themselves raised from the beggars that most of them were to the rank of the very wealthy. Our Masons have aspired to the glory of dying poor, but poor with villas, poor with palaces, poor with holdings, poor with many thousands they leave to their beneficiaries. Let's just glance at matriculated members of the sect rejoicing over most abundant pension which they accumulate without scruples; let's look at *masters of the lodge*, who have their hands in public administrations and take pinches of snuff that cost millions. Let's observe how *heroes* of the sect who were unable to resist the temptation of a gift of two million are immortalized with statues in all of the cities. Let's regard the sons of these *heroes*, who sell twice [the Isle of] Caprera and pocket huge sums, while deploring the prevailing misery. And our Freemasons won't even master all of the subtleties of the art of making money in like manner as the Hebrews do; but both together permanently master the art of snatching up much, for love of Italy.

So whoever attacks Masonry assaults Judaism, and whoever offends Judaism strikes the heart of Masonry. They have, in common, gluttony of gold and power, so they both feed on their envy of Christianity. Let's take the example of France. The war cry "Clericalism is the enemy" was conceived in the midst of the overflowing jewel cases of the Jew, Rothschild, and broadcast by way of Cousin, the Grand Master of Masonry, to [the Jewish Mason of high degree] Gambetta, who wore it on his sleeve. The fiercest chiefs of the crusade against *clericalism*, that is against the Christian Catholic religion, were a Dreyfus, a Herold, a Mayer, a Naquet, a Spuller, a Lockroy, an Ollendorff, altogether foreign Jews chosen as leaders by Freemasons. Among the most pitiless persecutors of Catholicism, the prize goes to the Jews Hendlé, Schnerb, and Levaillant. The Jew Sée invented the young girls' lycée, in order to de-Christianize, as much as possible, the French women. The Jew Giedroye mutilated the masterpieces of the classical authors, purging away from them the holy name of God, so that it would never come under the eyes of young scholars. The Jew Lyon-Alemand ended a teacher's career because that teacher had praised, in a book sent to be printed, the beneficial influence of Christianity on civilization. The Jew Naquet proposed the wicked law promoting divorce and saw to it that it was approved. The Jews tear down the crucifixes from the walls of the Paris schools, breaking them and giving orders to throw them into the sewers; and they defend, sword in hand, children's obligatory attendance of *secular* schools, that is of those without and against the Christian God. The Jews demand that the church of the Pantheon be

Part II ~ The Effects

desecrated, and at once this is granted to them. The Jews want to see the religious orders being banned from their houses, and the nuns from the hospitals, and immediately they are satisfied. The Jews sully France with the most obscene, most scandalous, most nauseous journalism imaginable, and the Freemasons eagerly disseminate it. In short, the Jews direct the work of destroying Christianity and every noble national tradition there, and the renegade Masons carry out this nefarious work with all their might.

We have mentioned the example of France. But we could look over all the other countries where the Jew is granted access to an unlimited enjoyment of civil rights. Everywhere, holding hands with the Freemasons, he insidiously reaches for the gold, and arms against the Christianity of the inhabitants. Even in the United States of America, abusing the freedom conceded them by the Republic of Washington, the Hebrews make themselves champions of the *neutral* public school, out of hatred of the Catholics, who wish to have free and Catholic schools for their children. With regard to this the *Freeman's Journal* has just raised a first cry of alarm, which we hope will not be fruitless.

The same can be said of our Italy, although aside from journalism, where they openly show themselves, the Jews operate more discreetly for the rest, throwing stones while hiding their hands. This very mount of ruins that the masonic revolution has amassed over thirty years, to Christianity's and Italy's corruption, is because of Judaism, that guides the sects of various types which have frequented its haunts. Mazzini flirted with the synagogue, and the fruits of these flirtations for the Capitol in Rome are well known. Garibaldi also flirted with the synagogue, as did Cavour, Farini, and Depretis. The synagogue's humble servants were and still are many of these *great* to whom the gullible public has erected or still erects busts and monuments so as to glorify their love of *liberty* and of the *fatherland*.

But it is superfluous to waste time proving a fact that is clearer than the noonday sun. Subsequently, we will indicate the ultimate goal which Judaism has in its eyes while operating in an anti-Christian manner and plundering, by means of Masonry.

This ultimate purpose is universal domination, is world domination, cherished as an article of faith by the degenerate cabbalists of Israel. As a respected personage has written in his book not long since:

> About thirty years ago, a little while before 1859, a prominent diplomat very well known in Vienna, from whose mouth we ourselves have heard this report, came to Europe from a South American capitol city, and traveling with him was the Brazilian minister for foreign affairs of that time, Grand Master of the masonic lodges of Brazil. The long and tedious passage caused the two statesmen to

strike up, in a certain way, a friendship. "You will see", the Grand Master said one day to the other, "that three great monarchies will develop in Europe, the Romanian one, under the House of Savoy, the German one, under the Hohenzollern, and the Slavic one, under the Romanov-Gottorf. These three monarchies will serve as transition to three great European republics, from which then will arise this great republic of mankind which is the aim of all the initiated brotherhood.[10]

Through the republic, Judaism everywhere wants to take a hold of power, under this same cover by which it has already taken a hold of it and exercises it unhinderedly in France.

Celebrating, in 1889, the first 100 year anniversary of the French Revolution, the Grand Orient Lodge of Paris held a Congress composed of representatives from two hemispheres, so that it could be called a *World Congress*. The acts of this clandestine council have sufficiently come to light with the speeches and toasts that were made there. On what point did most of the speakers dwell upon for their auguries, or better, their prophecies? Here it is: That the Christian world, 100 years after the upheavals of 1789, was lying in death's agony and, by the year 2000, would be finished off; that the destruction of monarchies and religious in those countries still immune to the benefits of 1789 ecstasies was imminent; that finally this universal republic would arise, whose arrival was drunk with wild enthusiasm.[11]/[28]

But as in the monarchies with their dynastic traditions the moral and civil patrimonies of the various nations meet in their center, and as the common religion is usually protected by the monarchies, which principle force of the states exists uniformly in all of the countries that are not subject to Masonry, thus with regard to them it is true also, that the struggle towards their ruin, in order to replace the solidity of the thrones with the fragility of government by the grace of the people, is of the greatest advantage for the aspirations of a race having neither a fatherland nor a public cult nor its own form of government, but living dispersed in all regions in order to subject them.

It is also noteworthy that the political, religious, and economic disorder, which in Europe is characteristically derived from the Jewish question, has produced this socialism which should stir the veins and increase the pulse of the Jews. For it seems that it is to be the terrible scourge of divine justice to crush the Jewish arrogance and, simultaneously, to make the Jews atone for their luciferian insolence.

---

[10] *Interessante Enthüllungen der Freimaurerei* [Interesting Revelations of Freemasonry], Vienna and Würzburg 1888.
[11] See *L'Univers* ["The Universe"], Paris, August 5, 1890.

PART III

THE REMEDIES

Some years ago, a French writer concluded one of his strong works on the Jewish invasion of his fatherland with an analysis that contained, in substance, what follows. The French Christians ought never to forget that these Jews with barbarian names and of barbarian origin, most of whom don't even possess citizenship, in less than a century have become our masters. Their invasion occurred in three phases: in that of 1791, when all of the national institutions collapsed; in that of 1815, when France fell prostrate; and in 1870, when the German weapons had mutilated France.

When in 1789 the era of revolution against the hegemony of the nobility and the clergy opened, what militated against these two ranks of our civilization and their ownership of two-thirds of French soil? Taine recently justified the origins of this ownership. The nobility had formed by defending the territory against the external enemies and thus procuring security and glory for the nation. The clergy had well deserved the credit for civilizing the nation, refining its customs and enriching it through scholarship, through monuments, and through thousands of different charitable institutions.

The clergy's possessions were estimated at about 4 billion. But in 1789 were counted at least 130,000 clergymen and religious in France. Consequently, the capital, divided up among them, was reduced to about 30,000 francs per person, thus to a profit of 1,500 per person. Accordingly, there was no question of great things, unless one had taken into consideration the great number of people who managed to live from these profits, and the innumerable alms they gave everywhere. In spite of this, such a legitimate patrimony was classified as an enormous abuse and confiscated.

A hundred years later, no longer 130,000 of our priests or religious, but 60,000 not at all French, but foreign, Jews, who constitute not at all a state illustrious for its excellent merits of the fatherland, but rather a voracious mob of immigrated cosmopolitans have snatched up, in our own house, not only 4 billion, but very well 90 billion.

And now, being lords over the public trust, they ardently desire to blind the common people, urging them against the clergy and thus hiding their monstrous wealth by means of the people's most wicked passions. Oh wonder, during the first revolution, the clergy were reproached with their 4 billion; and today, nobody wonders to see that the fortune of one single family of Hebrews (that of the Rothschilds), which has come in order to plunder us completely within a little more than sixty years, amounts to this same sum. What's more, this race, not content with bleeding us, makes every effort to kidnap from us the faith of Christ and all that is most beautiful in our culture!

Thus, in the end, the passionate French writer exclaimed:

> French Christians, let us unite to thwart the wicked conspiracy; let us form a defense league against these enemies of our name, our tribe, our beliefs and our patriotic traditions.

A similar cry begins to be heard in other countries, and might soon even arise in those where it is not heard yet, but will be heard ere long, when it won't help much any longer.

But will this defense league, whose formation is so much hoped for, really be one of the effective remedies for resolving the Jewish question, that with each passing day becomes more abominable for the people who languish, being oppressed and put in its chains?

Those who know their history realize that the problem of predominance of Jews over Christians is as old as Christianity itself. There is no country which wouldn't find recorded in its history a frequent change from permission for Jews to remain within its borders to their solemn expulsion, because of their abuses and misdemeanors. But up to our century, the Hebrew tribe was merely tolerated in the Christian kingdoms, being viewed with permanent suspicion as hostile, foreign and malevolent, and subject to special laws of exception, which constituted the common defense against their residing in those territories.

At present this is no longer the case. Thanks to the principles of the revolution, which he has used practically everywhere, the Jew has got the benefit of the common law: the law considers him equal to the others in all respects and protects him just as well as the other citizens. Thus the defense policy of Christian society has been abolished and the Jew has been granted the complete freedom to turn against the same societies which give him refuge in their midst.

Part III ∾ The Remedies

This is the most important conquest of *liberty*, which Judaism was able to obtain through Freemasonry, wherever it is subject to it and constitutes its ally.

But in order to make them last, the Jew has striven to eliminate everything that was historical and national in the institutions of the different states, by reducing all of them, some more and some less, except Russia, to such a form of government which was to insure that the bulk of power rested in the hands of the oligarchies, directly or indirectly depending upon him, as for instance, the modern parliaments, which pretend, through a continuous legal fiction, to govern in the name of national sovereignty but in fact impose on us the few who quite legally tyrannize all the others.

Once established as axioms of public law, the principles of equality for everyone in all things and the right of the predominating parties to govern the nation and the state without religion, Judaism was able through the instrument of Masonry to attain the apex of power which inebriates it and to dominate the Christian people in order to plunder, corrupt and trample them, as it is doing now in most of Europe.

Thus, the strongest weapon of defense against oppressive Judaism is broken in the Christians' fists, and as long as the insidious *rights of man*, promulgated in 1789, and the parliamentary statutes being in vogue today are maintained, there is no human hope for liberation of Christians from the Judaeo-Masonic yoke which wears down and perverts the populations.

Nevertheless, the previously quoted writer who invites Christians to band together in a defense league, justly demonstrates its necessity with these all too true words:

> Grasp it, Catholics, grasp it, all of you who, although you might not follow the religion of Jesus, are born Christians, that is, children of civilized parents: the Jews, barbarians still in the 19th century, keep their ancient offensive force, and they not only keep it, but increase it a hundredfold by their assaults through the breaches opened to them by the revolution, and certain of victory, they rush on us. And you, you have lost the right to defend yourselves; faced with an already half-victorious enemy, you have remained disarmed. Therein is the danger that arises a thousand times over the risks of our conflicts with prevailing Judaism in the past. By virtue of which principles or rights could the revolution ever repel its invasion? The state is atheistic or at least declares itself neutral towards the religions, and leaves the field not to the best one, but to that one which is the most audacious in plotting. Additionally the state has promulgated absolute equality of all citizens, unrestricted liberty, and, on this condition,

society turns into a tumultuary struggle between diverse and opposing forces, of which the most powerful will get the upper hand. And, unfortunately, the most powerful force is always the most malicious one, that in the choice of weapons doesn't even shrink from dishonesty.

This established, we wish to report, as already announced, upon some proposals by publicists who are not at all driven by socialist envy of the Hebrews' wealth, but rather animated with a zeal for religion and fatherland which, by the way, one would prefer being better moderated by justice. So, in Germany, Austria and France, there is a school of thought which advances a remedy for liberation from the Jewish plague, that, *per se*, would be the most radical of all, but that wouldn't conform to the Christian spirit and whose realization would be impossible at present.

After proving with hundreds of facts and documents that, in general, the Hebrews are a plague on Christian society, and a scourge on the Church of Jesus Christ, they demonstrate that the right of making war against them, as public enemies, is manifest. But since it doesn't beseem to resort to bloodshed, they restrict things which should be done to two points: That the Jew return what he has stolen; that he be banished from our territory afterwards. Through confiscation of his property and through exile the great evil done by him to the countries that have given him legal equality is to be recompensed and his pernicious ungratefulness towards their culture is to be punished.

That confiscation would be just, who can doubt? Most of the treasures possessed by the Jews are ill-gotten, gathered by fraud, usury, and embezzlement. If no end is imposed on this scandalous accumulation, then in a few decades almost all of the Christians' liquid and fixed assets will have fallen prey to them.

It is absolutely legitimate, if not always for particular individuals, then certainly for the plundered nation, to recover the ill-gotten gain from the thieves.

What else? Even if supposed but not admitted that the Jews' accumulated goods had been acquired justly, but also supposed that one has the legitimate right to wage war against them, then one has certainly the right, too, to impose upon them the lesser evil of confiscation. Add to this that gold is the most powerful weapon by which Jews exterminate religion and oppress the people; consequently, in regard to necessary defense, one has at least the right to seize this weapon from them.

And if one had no other reason, then nevertheless, one would have the right to compensation for the inestimable material and moral damages which they have done to the Christian people.

Part III ~ The Remedies

So here we have the case wherein the memorable sentence of the illustrious Peter the Venerable comes true: *Serviant populis christianis, etiam invitis ipsis, divitiae Judaeorum*: although unwillingly, give the benefit of the riches gathered by the Jews superabundantly to the Christians.

This first part of the remedy would result in what, some years ago at a meeting of anti-Semites, was expressed under the form of a wish: That to the Jews should be applied the very same laws which they themselves caused and allowed against the Church and promulgated by the Freemasons ruling in the Catholic countries. That by a decree of only two lines, all of the goods of the Jews, with no exception, be proclaimed *nationalized*. All at once there would be enough to pay off the public debts of the states.

It is not our intention to critically examine this formulated proposal more in depth. Suffice it to say that history abounds with examples of its implementation. But in order to be legitimate, first of all such a confiscation would have to be decreed by those who in the nations regularly exercise public authority. And secondly, it would have to be carried out according to a certain norm of justice and Christian charity. Not all of the Hebrews are thieves, swindlers, cheats, usurers, Freemasons, cads, and corrupters of customs. Everywhere one can count among them a certain number who are not complicit in the trickeries of the others. How could it be justified to include these innocents in the punishment deserved by the perpetrators?

The supporters of the drastic remedy answer that even in the most just and most holy wars, a great number of innocents also perish; that without distinction, all of the Hebrews act in solidarity with each other; that they altogether nurture a mortal hatred of the Christian in their hearts; that all of them, in one way or another, contribute to his destruction; that the experience of former times has shown how the Hebrew has always abused the mercy and charity of Christians, in order to take revenge and persecute them; and that consequently, this law of necessary self defense, which is not to be confounded with revenge, must take priority over every consideration. *Salus populi, suprema lex esto* [Let the people's welfare be the supreme law].

Since at present we are only dealing with a sketch, which for the present will certainly not be depicted more in detail, we'll leave it at that. Suffice it to add that, by all means, justice and charity would have to be vindicated for good reasons *versus* the rigor of its overly draconian measures.

But the confiscation would not be enough, the champions of that remedy insist; indeed, it would be of very little use if the common enemy was granted refuge on the state's own territory. One ought not to say: *Death to the Jew!* but rather, one ought to say: *Out with the Jew!* He may live, but far from us.

A French author writes:

> More than ten centuries is enough to prove that between our tribe and that of the Hebrews runs an incompatibility of humours that is totally insurmountable. We will never be able to live together without the greatest risks. Already in the epoch of the Renaissance, Bishop Simone Maiolo, in his famous book, *De perfidia Judaeorum* [On the Perfidy of the Jews], taught the Christians the only solution remaining for them in order to liberate themselves from these implacable enemies of their name, their fatherland, their faith, their peace, their goods, whom he called traitors, most felonious knaves of the human race, an army of quarrelers, rascals (*furciferi*), the scourge of decent men and unworthy of being tolerated. To concede to them, as did the revolution, the right of citizenship, was to unleash vampires on the country, was to open, out of a sentiment of humaneness, to a menagerie of ferocious beasts the doors of their cages. This race has no right to reside on our soil. If they are there, then it is either in order to take it away from us Christians, or in order to conspire to the detriment of our faith. We are faced with an enemy who aspires to deprive us of earth and heaven.

We limit ourselves to observing that, once more, the universal banishment of Jews from entire reigns and states has many examples. But the banishment was legitimate because it proceeded from the legitimate authority. If, by the way, this remedy had to be applied in all of the civilized countries, where on earth would be found a place for the eight million Jews who dispersedly squat everywhere?

"Let them go wherever they please," repeats the same writer; "their damnation is to wander forever as vagabonds." Well, then let them wander through the world. We shall not cease to repeat the ancient prayer of the holy liturgy:

> Auferte gentem perfidam
> Credentium de finibus.
> Remove the perfidious people
> from the believers' territory.

However much this wholesale banishment, as it would be called today, could be justified in certain circumstances and in particular countries, although in practice it wouldn't be universally feasible: it nevertheless contradicts the plans of God, Who through His prophets' mouths, has made the cursed Israel scattered to all parts of the world a palpable proof of Christianity's truth.

Otherwise has always been the attitude of the Church, of the Popes, and of the Catholic princes toward this people, who for almost twenty centuries

Part III ~ The Remedies

is afflicted with the curse of deicide: *Sanguis eius* (Jesu) *super nos et super filios nostros* [His blood (of Jesus) be upon us and upon our children],[1] as the synagogue of Caiphas called it down upon itself and its offspring.

Yet, citing the Lémann brothers who converted from Judaism:

> The Popes have always benevolently permitted the Hebrews to sojourn in their city. This errant people was free to go or not to go there, but it has always gone there, and in gratitude it called Rome *the Hebrews' Paradise*.

And the kings mostly imitated the Popes. They tolerated the Jews' presence in their states, but through wise laws protected the faith and possessions of their Christian subjects.

Even supposing that the remedy of universal banishment of the Hebrews was feasible now, it would not accord with the Roman Church's way of thinking and acting.

The followers of a more moderate school make various and more or less effective suggestions for driving back the Jewish hegemony, which nevertheless are very difficult to carry out at the present time.

Besides those suggestions of moral order concerning the relation of the Christians to the Hebrews, and the political ones regarding the freedom of press, the main force of Jewish power, as well as the tolerance of the masonic sect, they also present economic or social proposals, among which rank first those referring to the ownership of land and to so-called *capitalism*.

It is clear that the usurious loans granted by the Hebrews via real estate mortgages, year by year facilitate the transfer of the national territory from ownership by Christians to that by Hebrews. In Austria it is estimated that, in this way, about 10,000 farms fall into Jewish hands every year; in France, Italy, and elsewhere things don't look much different. If things will be going on like this, the point will be reached where the arable land of these various nations will turn into vast estates owned by a handful of foreign Croesuses whom the people will serve as slaves.

Now, here is the remedy for such a great evil that presents itself: a law composed of two simple, little articles: (1) Each foreigner is forbidden all ownership of rural land in the country; (2) Jews are equalized with foreigners.

The first article would be a completely just measure of defense and protection for the nation. Note, that the prohibition would be restricted solely to rural property: foreigners would still be allowed to own urban property. As to the second article, it would be required because of the peculiarity of the Jew, who, among us, is always a cosmopolitan, since he is, aside from the

---

[1] Matthew 27:20.

simple fact of being born in Germany, England or Italy, always but a Jew, and never a German, Englishman or Italian. And this cosmopolitanism of their tribe is admitted by the Jews themselves.

De Pascal had this to say:

> Thus it won't be helpful to resort to the dalliance of "equality" and "equal rights." To want *equal rights* under unequal social conditions is to want equal confections for unequal statures. What is just, what is necessary, what is equal, one of our great statesmen used to say, is equal respect for unequal rights. Our ancestors understood this quite well, and for this reason their edifice of state stood in a beautiful harmony after all, and not in this anarchy which is deplored today.[2]

But this external defense would have to be combined with a wise internal regulation of property, especially of the smaller and the quite tiny one, by means of which it would be protected from usury's eagerness for plunder. Wherever no such guarantees will be established, the proletariat of the cities will be overly crowded by those of the country: people who, loosed from the ties binding them to the soil, and left without fatherland, without roof, without bed, will fall into the hands of whoever will know how to exploit them in order to revolutionize society.

However, little would be won if at the same time one didn't arm, by good laws, against the abuses of *capitalism*, the main nerve of today's Jewish power in Europe. The so-called liberty of money transactions, behind which is hidden the most execrable infamies of usury, is tantamount to the ruin of the economic order of nations, as is the freedom of the press to their moral, political, and religious orders. Dr. Ratzinger justly states that:

> The expropriation of society, using fluid capital, is carried out with exactly the same precision as the laws of nature. If nothing is done to stop it, in 50, or at most, 100 years, all of European society will be abandoned, bound wrists and ankles, to the discretion of a few dozen Hebrew bankers.

It isn't necessary for our purposes to look into the particulars of the manifold reforms that this school, circumspectly, animated by the best intentions, and reconciling the rights of the Christian people with charity and justice due to the Hebrews, expounds and illustrates in order to free Christianity from the oppression inflicted by Judaism.

But as long as Christianity doesn't shed the political yoke of Masonry, it will be vain to propose and discuss possible solutions for liberation. The only solution and, at the same time the most reliable one, is to turn back and

---

[2] *Rome et les Juifs* [Rome and the Jews]

Part III ~ The Remedies

retake the way where one has gone astray. If the Hebrews are not put in their place by humane and Christian laws, certainly, but nevertheless by laws of exception which deprive them of *civil equality*, to which they have no right and which is even no less pernicious for them than it is for Christians, little or nothing will be accomplished. Seeing the inevitability of their presence in the various countries; seeing their unalterable nature of their being *foreigners* in every country, and of their being enemies of each country that tolerates them, and of their being a *society always separated* from the societies in which it lives; seeing the *Talmud's* morality that they follow, and the fundamental dogma of their religion which impels them to seize, by any means whatsoever, the goods of all peoples, because it assigns to their race the possession of, and the domination over, all the world; seeing that the experience of many centuries, and that one which we are undergoing at present, has proven and still proves, that the *legal equality* with Christians conceded to them in the Christian states results either in their oppression of Christians or in their slaughter by Christians, there emerges the consequence that the only way of reconciling the Hebrews' residence with the Christians' rights is to regulate it with such laws which, at the same time, impede the Hebrews from offending the Christians' welfare, and impede the Christians from offending that of the Hebrews.

And this is just what, in a more or less perfect manner, has been done in the past; this is what, for a century, the Hebrews have tried to abolish; but this is also what, sooner or later, willingly or unwillingly, will have to be restored, and perhaps the Hebrews themselves will be constrained to ask that it be restored. For the predominance to which today's revolutionary law has helped them is digging an abyss under their feet, whose depth corresponds to the height to which they have risen. And at the first burst of the storm they are provoking by their very predominance at present, they will suffer such an enormous ruin, heralding an event as unequaled in their history as their modern audacity is also unequaled and with which they have trampled the nations that have madly exalted them.

There is no lack of writers who opinion that the Jewish question is to be resolved by Israel's conversion to Christianity and that this is going to be that triumph for the Church which will prepare the end of the world. For one omen of end-times will precisely consist in the return of the Hebrews to the God handed over by them to the Cross on Calvary. This conversion, of which clear signs were already seen, would anew redound to the Church's advantage the immense wealth possessed by Judaism, and also the unlimited influence it exercises nearly everywhere now.

The Jewish Question in Europe

That the entry of apostate Israel into the sheep-fold of Christ be one of the signs given in Sacred Scripture as preceding the end of the world is beyond any doubt. But that the signs of such an entry would already show we wouldn't know how to become convinced of this. His dispersed and errant people, which always must exist, so that they testify to the belief in Jesus Christ, not only through the patrimony of the Scriptures they preserved, but also by their very condition, remain still today the same that they became after the destruction of Jerusalem: a people without a king, without a priesthood, without a temple, without a fatherland, without hope, and the most embittered enemy of the Name and the Church of Jesus Christ, Who was crucified by their ancestors. But that they would begin to take a turn for the better, and to embrace as their Savior, Jesus, Whom they have killed, of this we discern neither clear nor vague indications.

There are those who see such indications in the possession of the right of civil equality which it [*i.e.*, Israel] enjoys almost everywhere now. From this it follows, some claim, that many Jews have turned incredulous and profess no religion at all except that of the golden calf, and that many others, through their more liberal intermingling with the Christian, have been brought near to the Church, whose bosom at present they enter without making a great stir, but in considerable numbers. If we limit ourselves to what is visible and palpable and what we have proven at length, it seems to us that it can be said that equality conceded to the Hebrews by the anti-Christian sect [*i.e.*, Freemasonry], wherever it has usurped the government of the peoples, has produced the effect of uniting Hebraism with Freemasonry in the persecution of the Catholic Church, and of elevating the Jewish race in its occult power as well as in its manifest abundance of wealth over the Christians. That not a few Israelites become Protestant, or rather feign joining the nationalistic Christianity of the Lutherans, Calvinists, Anglicans, and so on, is well known, but it is also well known that they are induced to these feigned conversions by everything except religious reasons. That others turn from the synagogue to Catholicism may be authentic in case they do so secretly; but exactly because being done secretly, such conversions do not suffice at all for constituting a recognizable sign.

In every century, for the rest, God has attracted, in varying measure, considerable numbers of Jews to His Church, sometimes more, sometimes less, and it would not be proper to compare the converts of our time with those of past epochs. But it is certain that at present, Judaism, taken as a whole, shows itself incomparably more inclined to hatred and suppression of Christianity than to benevolence toward it and its edification. And the satanism because of which Masonry has waged its campaign against all of

Part III ~ The Remedies

what it knows to be Catholic, isn't nurtured more insidiously by anything other than by the Israelites' pen, machinations, suggestions and gold.

Thus, if the resolution of the Jewish question in Europe had to be postponed until the mission of Enoch and Elias, we think that before there would still be enough time to see Europe become, for long centuries, one single, huge plantation, exploited by the Jews through the labor and sweat of the Christians reduced to slavery. Accordingly, this is no remedy in which we can acquiesce, since it is, on the one hand, too fantastic, and on the other, too remote.

What must be the true solution of the problem, and the radical cure for the Jewish disease in Europe, has been clearly demonstrated, as has also been demonstrated the practical impossibility to resort to this cure as long as there are governments which continue to replace the ten commandments, the faith, and the Gospel of Christ with the principles glorified by the French revolution. If the Christian societies, having been removed from the Church of Jesus Christ, won't return to Her, they will wait in vain for their liberation from the iron yoke of the Jews. As long as sin will endure, punishment also will endure and even intensify.

The Greeks' apostasy was punished by the Mohammedans, who destroyed their empire. Heaven's chosen instrument of anger for punishing the degenerate Christianity of our time is the Hebrews. Their power over Christianity is continually increasing, along with the predominance of that evil spirit in it that followed up the rights of God with the *rights of man* in its bosom. The justice of the Eternal makes use of the most apostate and most cursed people in order to scourge the apostasy of the nations more favored by His mercy.

France sets an example of this. She has just celebrated the first centenary of that revolution which separated her from God, the Church, and her kings. But how did she celebrate this solemnity? France prostrated herself in the dust of the Masonic temple of Solomon, humiliated under the feet of the talmudic synagogue, as a slave of a swarm of foreign vultures who have already drained three fifths of her ancestors' patrimony from her. And thus, the revolution of 1789 has yielded her the glorious profit of passing from the noble submission to her most Christian kings over to the ignoble servitude of the kings of Mammon.

Different from France is Italy. She is that country to whom, for quite thirty years, more than to the other nations, Freemasonry has instilled the poison of those liberties which have nearly killed France. And the effects seem most deplorable, not only in political, economic, or moral aspects, in which she resembles her elder sister more and more, but also in the enslavement to the ghetto, which by means of Masonry brings Italy under its subjection more each year.

Well, let there form leagues of Christians who want somehow to stop the flood of Judaism that rushes in and, being free from any restraint, devastates along with the material wealth also the most previous treasures of our faith and our civilization; well, let the people disseminate the idea of the necessity for public welfare, to confine this pernicious river to its ancient bed again, by just laws; let the people write, print, speak, struggle towards that, always within the limits permitted by the Gospel. But let no one who possesses genuine love of religion and of his country become weary, everywhere, again and again, of continually driving in the nail of this great truth: that for the nations who have jointly apostatized from the Church in order to follow the masonic pretences, modern Hebrews constitute the scourge of divine justice, and that the whole sweetness of liberalism will result in their being lured into the embrace of the voracious octopus of Judaism.

Toussenel, Proudhon, Lafargue, and a hundred others predicted what would necessarily be the resolution of the Jewish question in Europe. As the barbarians from outside resolved the Jewish question of the most decayed Roman world, thus the barbarians from inside will resolve the present one which has arisen from the so-called reigning or bourgeois class that has been seduced, inebriated, and corrupted to the marrow by Judaism. Hasn't it refused, out of hatred for Christ, any social reform that was based on Christian justice as its basis? Well, the new Attila will be unleashed upon their republics, their monarchies, their institutions, their stock exchanges, their theaters, their factories, their places of entertainment, and he will bring them to ruin along with the Jews. Haven't they jointly repudiated the Lord's Anointed? They will jointly take delight in Barabbas. And when Barabbas will have treated them as they deserved, the Lord's Anointed will return to His house and demonstrate that it remains true forever: that whoever raises his horn[s] against Him will, being conquered, end up licking the dust of His feet—*pulverem pedum tuorum lingent*.[3]

---

[3]   Isaias 59:23.—We have just learned that the Italian translation of Martinez' book, *The Jew, Here's the Enemy*, with annotations for Italy, is already in press and may soon be published.

NOTES TO THE ROMAN NUMERALS

*The roman numerals in the text
and the following notes were added by the Translator.*

[i]. We see this in the 20th century rise of National Socialism. 19th Marxism was converted in Heaven to German Socialism and 19th century Zionism into German Nationalism. Rabbi Eichanan Wasserman, in *Epoch of the Messiah* (copyright 1985 by Rabbi E.S. Wasserman, Los Angeles, CA 90069) writes:

> Nowadays, Jews have chosen two [idols] to which they offer up their sacrifices. They are Socialism and Nationalism. The new gospel of Nationalism can be defined briefly as "Let us be like the nations." All that is required of the Jew is national feeling. He who pays the Shekel and sings Hatikvah is thereby exempted from the precepts of the Torah. It is clear that this idea is considered to be fundamentally idol-worship from the point of view of the Torah. These forms of idol-worship have poisoned the minds and hearts of the Hebrew Youth. Each one has its tribe of false prophets in the shape of writers and speakers, who do their work to perfection. A miracle has happened in Heaven: these two idolatries have been merged into one—National Socialism. There has been formed from them a fearful rod of wrath which hits at the Jews in all corners of the globe. The abominations to which we have bowed down strike back at us. "Thy sin shall punish thee."

Thus, National Socialism was invented in Heaven as a measure-for-measure punishment to the Jews for their perfidy. Here *La Civiltà Cattolica* is prophetic.

A similar interpretation to that of Rabbi Wasserman's treating Hitler as a kind of Attila punishing the Jews for their sins is from Rabbi Avigdor Miller in his tape number 347 [Rabb Miller Tapes, 2002 Avenue J, Brooklyn, New York 11210]. Rabbi Miller in this tape considers Adolf Hitler a Providential punishment on the Jews for their sins. Another work by I. Domb, entitled, *The Transformation*, is available from *The Jewish Guardian* [P.O. Box 2143, Brooklyn New York, 11202].

[ii]. We would say more than ninety percent of the *Talmud* is pharisaical. See "Commentary on Terms."

[iii]. See *Genesis 9:27*.

[iv]. Those comments of the Rabbis of today are not found in the 6th century Gemara itself, but their Pharisaical views are considered by them as one tradition with the Talmud.

[v]. The messianism can be found in various Jewish apostasies completely unconnected to the Bible. First is the usury system that underlies all modern Jewish power. That this system, as all non-Biblical systems, is a death system, was demonstrated by Aristotle in his *Politics*, 1:3:23. Once all the gold in the system is lent out, the gold cannot generate its own children or liquidity to pay the interest. For example, if 140,000 tonnes of gold are lent out at 10%, and there are only 140,000 tonnes of gold in the world, it is impossible that 154,000 tonnes of gold could be paid at the end of the year when it is due. The 14,000 tonnes of gold would not exist. Defaults follow. So, the Jewish usurer in the Middle Ages gathered all the nation's wealth into his hands until he was expelled. St. Thomas Aquinas, in *The Summa Theologica,* in "Of the Sin of Usury," (Q 78, Art 1, Part 11-11) wrote: "I answer that, to take usury for money lent, is unjust in itself because this is to sell what doesn't exist …"

The 18th and 19th centuries introduced, via Jewish usurers such as the Rothschilds, the fraudulent paper and credit systems as described by J. W. von Goethe in *The Tragedy of Faust*, Part 2. Here the liquidity, or children, were artificially created in the form of paper and credit to service the interest, but this system is also against nature and God as it fraudulently creates value out of nothing. (See *Lev. 19:36* that legislates against this fraud; *Ex: 22:25; Lev. 25:36,37,* and *Deut. 23:19, 20* for usury prohibitions.) Since the usury relentlessly continues to accumulate, the paper and credit must continuously be created by the central and the private banks to pay the interest until the system becomes so fractionalized that it disintegrates, as in Germany between 1914-1923.

As this fractionalization took place, the Rothschilds "manipulated the quantity and flow of money so that they were able to influence, if not control, governments on one side and industries on the other." (*Tragedy and Hope,* page 51, by Carroll Quigley, 1966, The Macmillan Co., N.Y.). If the Rothschilds wanted to get rid of a government, they would contract the supply of credit through their controlled central bank, creating a depression and political upheaval, as the Parisian Baron Edouard de Rothschild did between 1929-1932 in the United States to get rid of the protectionist Republicans who were moving to disrupt their international loans. Of course, they sell their asset portfolio before the crash, and buy back the assets afterwards. The enormous wealth thus accumulated is used to foster such heresies as Talmudic Ricardianism, Talmudic Darwinism, Talmudic Marxism, Talmudic Freudianism, and Talmudic Einsteinism, which will be treated in further footnotes. Therefore, *fiat* currency and credit are merely pharisaical control mechanisms.

[vi]. In Hebrew, *goy* means nation, and can refer in the Hebrew *Bible* to the Israelite nation, but in the *Talmud*, it refers mostly to non-Jews.

[vii]. Russian independence from Jewish financial control was ended by a calculated series of events started by Parisian Baron Edouard de Rothschild who

Translator's Notes

arranged the assassination of Archduke Ferdinand of Austria at Sarajevo in 1914 to draw the weak Russian state into a European war to end the Tsarist regime. It was rather surprising to the Parisian Baron that the Russian Tzar held on so long, which forced him into planning the Bolshevik Revolution in 1918 by having his Agent, Parvus, engineer through the German government the transfer of Lenin in a sealed railway car from Switzerland to Russia with his Jewish crew. The later suppression in the western press of the atrocities being committed in Russia was carried out by the Rothschild forces as Russia fell under a Jewish dictatorship more ruthless, brutal and murderous than anything ever before seen in history. We refer to the recently published *Black Book of Communism* for a detailed account.

[viii]. Historically, many of these rights and privileges were given through Jewish bribery of the aristocracy, or of public officials.

[ix]. The so-called political economists as David Ricardo or Milton Friedman are essentially Talmudic apologists for economic doctrines of the cut-throat competition used in an economic contraction to consolidate and monopolize industries under Jewish private banking control. These economic doctrines were applied by Charles Darwin to the survival of the fittest doctrine and natural selection. The Jewish newspapers touted Talmudic Darwinism as a means to destroy the Biblical basis of Christian civilization. The vile idea that man emerged from an animal has never been witnessed by the human eye, but was nevertheless used to destroy God's account of Adam and Eve. The Jews were confounded when, in our century, Adolf Hitler turned the tables on them and characterized them as the inferior species unfit to survive and slated them to be destroyed as the Jewish Bolsheviks like Kaganovich had liquidated the 10 million Christian families in the Ukraine in the Kulak class liquidations; and so the Jews were punished measure-for-measure. It is important to note that, just as Talmudic sexology is contrary to Scripture, reason and natural law, so is Darwin's *Descent of Man* contrary to Scripture and empirical natural evidence (*i.e.,* what we can see).

[x]. Here is an appropriate place to discuss the Jewish sexual science, Talmudic Freudianism.

The philosophy can be found in the homosexual, Oscar Wilde's, *The Picture of Dorian Gray*, the part in which Lord Henry Wotton proclaims: "The only way to get rid of a temptation is to yield to it." Dr. Freud's contention is that repression of the sexual urge causes mental illness. In the movie, "Splendor in the Grass," made some decades ago, Natalie Wood, who plays the lead, ends up in the Kansas Meninger Hospital for resisting sex on a date, while the fornicating girls are depicted as emotionally healthy.

During my visits to the Meninger Hospital, my discussions with both doctors and patients found no patients there suffering because of holy continence. Rather, I found most girls suffering from guilt and disorientation caused by sexual misdeeds. The Talmudic Freudian psychiatrists' goal there was to free the patients from illness by taking away the guilt of their sins. Here is the new Jewish monastery, a whorehouse, and the priesthood, psychiatrists. Their mystery, as in the evolutionism of Darwinism, is the (unseen) *unconscious*.

During the 1930s, Dr. Carl Jung answered the Freudians, who based their sexology on the unconscious Oedipus complex archetype, by saying the racial national spirit of Adolf Hitler and the German people came from their unconscious and was the German archetype, while the Jewish archetype was the Oedipus complex. This is a rather farcical game, as the unconscious is, by definition, unknown.

Unfortunately, Freud dominates our school systems and a perfidious sex education is taught, promoting vices such as masturbation, sodomy and kindred perversions.

[xi]. The school texts are infected with Talmudic Einsteinism and Marxism. It is easy to see that Karl Marx's ideas are foolish, since he tries to create equality of result instead of equality of opportunity, thereby destroying all incentives. God divided the land of Israel equally (*Numbers: 26:54*), but not the fruits of the work (*Prov. 20:4*). We wonder why the Rothschilds and other Jewish plutocrats desire to concentrate so much wealth when the Bible's equality of landholding and the Jubilee (*Lev. 25:25-28*) prevented such permanent concentration, except that we know that this is their tool for one-world domination. And, of course, the answer is that they are rebels against the Bible and God, so no monstrosity is beyond their luciferian plotting.

Dr. Einstein is less easy to understand. Suffice it to say that our eyes see that the earth is not moving and the sun orbits the earth. Galileo never proved otherwise, but his "theory" that the Bible's geocentricity was wrong, using meaningless, disconnected empirical data promoted the empirical movement, which encouraged the idea that truth could be found by examining a stupendous number of facts, and that the patterns of fact could challenge the Bible. This was contrary to the Aristotelian method of investigation which searched for the nature of the problem and once found, used the analysis to organize the empirical data somewhat as theories do today. But Aristotle used deductive logic from things that were real and known, rather than inferential logic from things unknown as Plato and today's scientists.

Here is an example. When Aristotle observed that a baby was born from a man and a woman, he deduced that in the past that was always the way. He saw what was real and deduced conclusions from it. However, the Darwinists see a scale of species, and infer one species was born from another, though they never saw such a thing. (The ancients had such beliefs, as Helen of Troy being born from a swan's egg, which today would be called a form of *punctuated equilibrium*.) The Darwinists then launch into gigantic empirical data searches to prove linkages through graded species, though there is no visible evidence one was born from the other, and become lost in the confusion of data. Aristotle's method saves us from becoming detoured into such irrelevant data searches which have encumbered our entire educational system which murders the innocent souls of our children with millions of irrelevant "facts." We are sure the Pharisees want this intellectual confusion to facilitate their control. So, they never proved a pattern of facts that could repudiate Biblical creation, but merely showed the differing species that God created on an ascending scale, and called it evolution. You could just as easily say the scale indicated the descent of the species and call it de-volution. The connection between these species is never proved as having evolved because no one ever saw one come out of another, and thus modern science is counter-intuitive.

In 19th century science, it was held that air carried the voice and that in a theoretical vacuum there could be no conversations. As a corollary, it was believed (even before the time of Sir Isaac Newton) that the aether carried light waves as air carried sound. While the aether could not be proved, it was considered as a theory scientifically logical as a corollary to sound transmission via the air. Towards the end of the 19th century, experiments were performed by an interferometer by sending light waves in the direction the earth was alleged to be moving, vertically, and in reverse, to prove the earth's movement by measuring the resistance of the aether wind. These experiments demonstrated that there was no aether wind resistance, and using scientific logic thus there was no earth movement. It is important to point out that scientific logic and absolute proof are not the same. But, then, in almost all astronomy, there is no absolute proof. Dr. Einstein's contribution to this problem was to try to save appearances for atheism by saying there was no aether.

Einstein believed in the God of Spinoza, who postulated that the universe and all the people in it were God, which represents such an irrational insanity that we can safely call them atheists. Think, dear reader, of all the bad things men do and then consider, as did Einstein and Spinoza, that this too is God. See Pierre Bayle's analysis of Spinoza in his *Dictionaire historique et critique*. The most important lesson that can be drawn from this discussion is that neither heliocentricity nor a-centricity can be absolutely proved by science, since they base their conclusions on unobserved phenomena. The *Bible*, therefore, has not been disproved, and so, all schools teaching Einstein, Galileo or Darwin are undermining God's infallible words with unproved teachings. It is by this rebelling against God that Christians have become prone to the Jewish degenerate doctrines and thus have been punished by God by the Jewish plague. God will end this perfidy, as He did in Germany, in His good time unless they repent.

Let us pray, dear reader, that this translation of the 1890 *Civiltà* 3-part series helps them along the path of true reform.

TRANSLATOR'S NOTE

This Translator's Note by the same contemporary anonymous translator who added the 11 Roman numeral endnotes, provides an historical background for the *La Civiltà Cattolica* thesis and contributes to an understanding of the Talmudic terms used by the Jesuits in that 1890 3-part series.

Many do not realize that most Jews who live among us are not the people of the *Old Testament*. While most Jews living in the United States would identify themselves as *Reformed* or *Conservative* Jews (which erroneously implies an amending of earlier errors of interpretation), these two Jewish branches essentially follow the Talmudic psychology of applying human inventions to replace divine Scripture. Therefore, these two branches—most of whose constituents favor abortion, birth control, and homosexual rights—have little to do with the *Old Testament*.

Orthodox (Talmudic) Jews, referred to as Pharisaic Jews in the *New Testament*, ostensibly recognize the Divine authenticity of the *Old Testament* but add to and subtract from these laws, as their so-called oral law dictates. When they organized this oral law in the written *Talmud*[1] (if this maze can be called "organized"), they asserted that this lengthy legal addition was given by God to Moses at Mt. Sinai at the same time the written *Pentateuch* was dictated.

While it would be highly questionable that such a lengthy 2700-page small print treatise could be remembered over that 1700 year period merely through oral transmission, it is also highly illogical, as this oral tradition contradicts the written law, adding at will to or subtracting from Biblical laws. It is impossible for a student to study this amalgam and be able to make heads or tails of it.

The *Talmud*—which consists of the 6th century *Mishna*, or repetition, and the 6th century *Gemara*, or completion—follows Justinian's format in that the *Mishna* would be the Institutes, or elements, or first principles of a no longer oral law, while the *Gemara* would be the Pandects or digests, containing the opinion of learned Rabbinical doctors, except that the *Gemara* is not digested

---

[1]. There are two *Talmuds*, one of which was written in Babylon and the other in Jerusalem. The Rabbis consider the Babylonian one authoritative.

in a systematic method. Using the ostensible style of the Socratic dialectic, questions are asked in one part and can be answered hundreds of pages later. It is largely incoherent and often vile and obscene.

Even learned Rabbis tell us that without the commentary of Rashi, the *Talmud* cannot be understood. Rashi is an acronym for Rabbi Solomon, son of Isaac of Troyes (1040-1105), who is sometimes also found under the name of Yarchi or Jarchi, meaning "moon" in Hebrew, having been connected by some to a French city named Lunes, or moon in English.

Other Rabbis, relying on Rashi and others, wrote the code books interpreting the interpretations of the *Talmud*, and so the so-called people of the book present us with untold millions of words of their own opinions,[2] most of which have nothing to do with the *Old Testament*. This incessant insectile noise drowns out the true words of the *Bible* that are of divine origin.

The part of the *Talmud* called the Gemara contains tractates such as Bava Metzia, or middle gate. This deals with the laws of moveable property and wages. Bava Kama, or first gate, deals with laws regarding torts or damages. And Bava Bathra, or final gate, deals with laws involving real property.

Berakhot, or blessings, is a tractate treating prayers and blessings. Rosh Hashana, or head of the year, or new year, deals with the New Year (a holiday described in the *Pentateuch* as the first day of the seventh month, and in *Ezekiel 40:1* as Rosh Hashana) and the calendar. Sanhedrin, or great council, deals with the judiciary system.

The code books seek to classify this stupendous amalgam of laws numbering over 11,000 statutes. The *Pentateuch* has only 613, over half of which cannot be observed by them and apply to the non-existent Temple. It is important to note that less than 300 apply today, on an *Old Testament* basis, in contrast to the *Talmud's* over 11,000.

To master these codes requires endless study. The main one is entitled, Shulchan Aruch (spread on the table). The Schulchan Aruch is the standard code of Jewish law, written by Rabbi Joseph Caro (1488-1575), and has, as

---

[2]. The blinded Rabbis established the right to add these millions of words, based on one small Hebrew word in the *Pentateuch* (Pi) which signified mouth. It is found in *Exodus 34:2-7*. But the word is an expletive particle, denoting the manner and value of anything, as appears from *Genesis 43:7* and *Leviticus 27:18* and therefore should be rightly translated "the tenor" of those words. Yet, their Rabbi Johannes, in the very beginning of Halicoth Olam (Eternal Way), gathers from here that God made a covenant now with their Fathers, concerning all the unwritten laws delivered by word of mouth. As long as they adhere to this opinion, they can never understand their divine writings. For what can be more plain that the Covenant here mentioned was ordered to be written. We have elaborated on the Talmudic legalistic methodology in this footnote so the reader can understand this important point more clearly.

Translator's Notes

one of its four parts, Chochen Mishput, meaning the breastplate of judgment worn by the high priest.

The reference to Kol Nidre refers to a prayer said by Jews on the evening of the holiest day of the year, the Day of Atonement—and which means the voice of vowing. It asks God to forgive the Jews for vows that they may make in the coming year and then break. This is asking forgiveness in advance.

These codes teach lay Jews many things not found in Scripture. Examples: (1) unemployed Jews must have sexual intercourse with their wives every night except during the roughly twelve days of menstruation,[3] which we find in the *Bible* as seven days, even though the *Bible* not only requires but limits sexual intercourse for procreation (see St. Augustine's, *On the Good of Marriage*); (2) how to illegally get around the laws of debt release required at the end of every Sabbatical year; (3) that milk and meat cannot be eaten together, although the *Bible* only forbids boiling a kid in his mother's milk; and (4) the treating of all non-Jews under the severe disabilities of Canaanites, though this obviously has no basis in the *Bible*.

The Canaanite treatment is found in *Deuteronomy 7:2-5,* whereby these seven nations were condemned to death for unnatural sexual vice, incest, and other abominations found in *Leviticus 20*. While this misapplication of the law to apply to descendants of Japheth (Western Europeans) is found throughout the *Talmud*, it is brought forward in the code book of Maimonides, under *The Book of Knowledge* 78[a], translated as follows:

> But as regards the Minoans (heretics) and Epicureans (heretics), it is a commandment to destroy them with your own hand and throw them into the pit of destruction for they persecute Israel and seek to turn them away from their God, as Jesus the Nazarite and his followers, as well as Zodok (Sadducees) and Boethius (Sadducees) and their followers, may their name rot.

---

[3]. The depraved Jewish marriage laws extend, even requiring similar frequent sexual intercourse, into pregnancy and nursing (see *Code of Jewish Law, Kitzur Schulchan Aruch*, or abbreviated table spread, Hebrew Publishing, 1961, NY, Volume 4, Chapter 150, page 15, item 7). It can thus be seen what a grave error it was to let the Jews out of the Ghetto, for this opened onto Western Civilization a veritable floodgate of sensuality. Noteworthy in this regard is contemporary Talmudic Freudianism. By disconnecting sexuality from procreation, the Jews have demonstrated that they have fallen into carnality, as St. Augustine had taught. While the Jewish-American Anti-Defamation League (ADL) kills God in the public schools by banning school prayer and *Bible* reading, or puts into the schools Professor Eli Weisel's books calling for the trial of God (see *Matthew 27*), the Jewish *New York Times* demands condoms for the students who have been corrupted by the ADL culture which promotes homosexual rights. The *Talmud* also sanctions artificial birth control under certain circumstances.

The Jewish Question in Europe

It is noteworthy that not only Christians are to be treated as Canaanites but also Sadducees and Boethians. These latter are called today Karaites, who try to adhere only to the written law of the *Bible*. For this they have earned the undying hatred of the Talmudists, but have generally been recognized as good citizens in the countries of western Europe. The German government, during 1933-1945, exempted the Karaites from persecution, showing how Providence delivers the good from the flames of punishment as Shadrach, Mesdach, and Abed-nego in *Daniel 3*. (See *Encyclopedia Judaica Jerusalem*, Vol. 10, page 775.)

These erroneous interpretations have filled history with blood. The Jewish rebellion against Rome, put down in 70 AD by Titus, and the so-called Bar Kokbba (son of the star rebellion or the Messianic rebellion according to Rabbi Akiba) put down by Hadrian in 132 A.D., stem from this implacable Rabbinical hostility to all mankind. We find in *Epitome* (Book 68:32), Dion Cassius claims that the Jews "would eat the flesh of their victims, make belts for themselves of their entrails, anoint themselves with their blood, and wear their skins for clothing."[4]

This Talmudic spirit has been carried forward in our century where the Jewish Bolsheviks, such as Lazar Moiseyevich Kaganovich, between 1928-1932, carried out the liquidation through starvation of 10 million men, women and children during the Kulak extermination in the Ukraine. We have similarly found the American Jewish Anti-Defamation League promoting abortion rights in the U.S., leading to the killing of 60 million unborn babies.

What happened in Germany during the 1933-1945 may now be more understandable to the reader as the Providential punishment the Jews suffered, as predicted in *Deuteronomy 28*. While we pray for the repentance of the Jews, we can only see the repeat performance of the 1930's if they pursue their present course. May God grant them the wisdom to understand the consequences of their actions and the strength to act accordingly.

---

[4]. *Encyclopedia Judaica of Jerusalem*, Volume 5, page 39, tells us the papyri confirms the account of Dion Cassius.